Glass
Art Nouveau and Art Deco

Studio Vista
Christie's

Glass
Art Nouveau and Art Deco

Albrecht Bangert

Christie's South Kensington Collectors' Guides

A production of Plenary
Publications International, Amsterdam

Series editor: Albrecht Bangert
Design: Joerk Reitz
Translation: Dan Klein

A Studio Vista book published
by Cassell Ltd,
35 Red Lion Square, London, WC1R 4SG
and at Sydney, Auckland, Toronto, Johannesburg,
an affiliate of
Macmillan Publishing Co., Inc., New York

ISBN 0 289 70869 9
Filmset in Great Britain by TNR Productions, London
Printed and bound by Grijelmo, S.A., Bilbao, Spain

1 *Victoire* ('Victory'). Moulded glass
car mascot by René Lalique in
clear glass with a satin finish - also
known as 'Spirit of the Wind'.
15 × 26 cm, *c.* 1928.

Contents

Introduction to Art Nouveau and Art Deco

Probably the most decorative period of glass design that there has been was between the years 1890 and 1930. The first part of this period from 1890-1914 is popularly known in England as Art Nouveau, in Germany as *'Jugendstil'* and in France quite simply, as *'Dix-neuf-cent'*. The style that followed it in the 1920s and the 1930s (a style no less decorative and appealing than its predecessor), is known in England and Germany as 'Art Deco', an abbreviation taken from the French title of the 1925 World Exhibition of decorative arts in Paris, *'Les Arts Décoratifs et Industriels Modernes'*; in France however it is more common to refer to it as *'Le Style '25'*. Abandoning earlier traditions glass designers gave free rein to their fantasy, producing glass forms which were almost surrealist in concept, in an effort to escape from merely

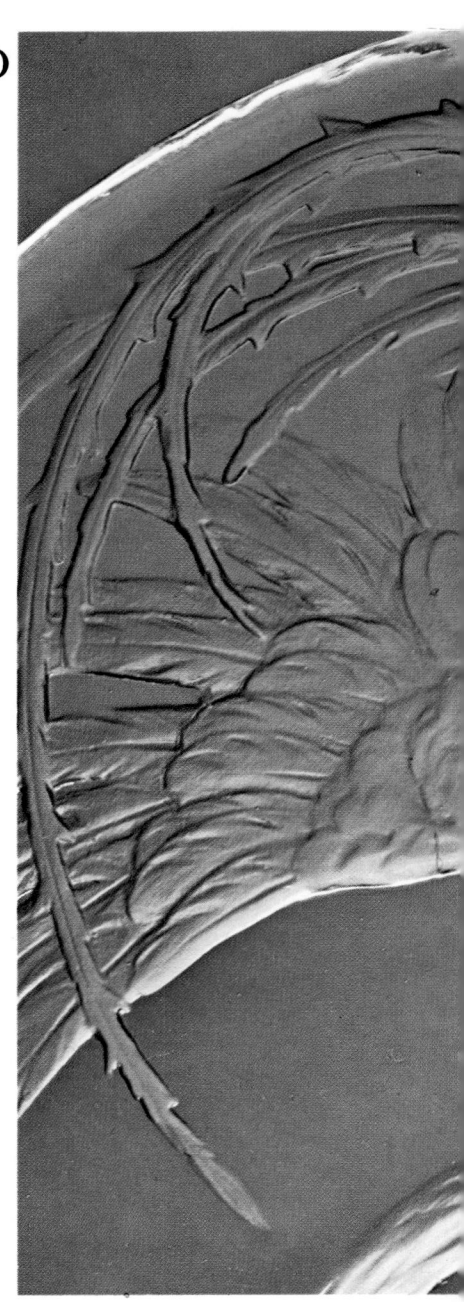

2 *L'Oiseau de Feu'* ('The Firebird'). 'Light sculpture' in clear glass by Lalique. This solid glass panel is 32 cm high and sits on a bronze base. The strange 'firebird' creature is deeply engraved which gives a three dimensional effect. It is signed 'R. Lalique' and was produced during the 1920s.

functional designs.

During the Art Nouveau period glass designers freed themselves of the stylistic clutter of earlier times; they liberated themselves from all practical considerations and unashamedly saw decoration as an end in itself. In their spirit of new-found freedom they found inspiration not so much in antiquity as in the properties inherent in glass itself; the potential of glass had up till then remained unexplored and un-exploited. They became fascinated by the natural iridescence of a piece of glass a thousand years old, and by the geometric shapes in that iridescence, formed by the actions of plants and insects and by encrusted stones.

The golden hoard discovered by the archaeologist Schliemann, and later finds in Tutankhamen's tomb, must have been partly responsible for the gold lustre effects developed by European and American glass craftsmen of the period. Also newly discovered natural substances, as well as the new shapes and colours of cubism and other art movements, tended on the whole to fire the artist's imagination more than the old-fashioned academism still being taught in colleges of art.

In their search for inspiration, artists looked to oriental art, and its long-established treatment of the animal and plant worlds; this influence is apparent in the curved animal designs, flower forms and landscape decoration of French Art Nouveau cameo glass.

During the Roman era, glass was already appreciated as an art form, and the tradition of glass-collecting is as old as glass itself. The Roman historian Pliny refers, even at this early stage, to the tremendous value of fine art glass, when he describes how the Emperor Nero paid the princely sum of 6000

3 Gallé showcase, designed by him for the 1900 Paris World Fair and used to display his work.

sesterces for two pieces of glass on account of their extraordinary shimmering iridescence.

Art Nouveau Past and Present

Even at the time of its manufacture (around 1900) Art Nouveau art glass was seriously collected, but during the course of the last decade it has enjoyed a spectacular boom in price on the international art market.

For the uninitiated, Art Nouveau glass is a complex subject; the

by English lead-crystal and Bohemian chalk-glass. The Art Nouveau glass artists attached no importance to such criteria. For them glass was a substance whose qualities went far beyond simple transparency. Art Nouveau glass makers used organic shapes to express poetic ideas as they found the substance and colour properties of glass expressive in themselves. They looked to nature for inspiration and found it in the

4/5 Various overlay and *'Marqueterie de Verre'* vases by Gallé.

merits of an artist-signed piece are judged on a combination of colour, shape and technical craftsmanship. The most prized pieces are those in which artists evolved hitherto untried techniques, even if this involved upsetting long-established principles of glass design. Before this period glass manufacturers were not attracted by the possibilities of coloured glass; the qualities they looked for and prized in glass were clarity and crystalline transparency, epitomised

changing seasons and in the birth, growth and decay of the plant world. Their philosophy of art made use of the elements (earth, fire, air, water), and of the arbitrary way they could cause chemical change. Art Nouveau glass designers relied on impulse, creative imagination and originality and ignored convention. Such observations might still lead one to ask why they decided to ignore tradition and break away from the former obsession with crystalline clarity. By returning to nature in this way and with their self-consciously 'Primitive' treatment of glass, these artists were protesting against the ever increasing effects of industrialization and its oppressive influence on civilised man and society.

Art Nouveau was in effect an artistic protest against the technical perfection sought by an industrial age. At the turn of the century Louis Comfort Tiffany, the American glass designer, developed techniques which gave his glass a shimmering iridescence, like the patina on a piece of glass a thousand years old. In France, Emile Gallé wanted his glass to express romanticism and the pathos of poetry, and in Germany, Karl Koepping fashioned glass in flower forms of extraordinary delicacy.

L'Exposition Universelle 1900 Paris

The spring of 1900 saw the official 'birth' of Art Nouveau, with the World Fair held in Paris that year. This much-heralded and elaborately staged moment of birth seems also to have been the artistic peak of Art Nouveau! Thereafter there were no significant stylistic developments: the new wealth of ideas became commercially exploited, although this was directly opposed to the fundamental beliefs of an art movement that was against industrialism. The Exhibitors who showed their wares at the *Exposition Universelle* were richly rewarded with medals and prizes for their work; drunk with success they turned their attention to business opportunities, and, unable to resist the lure of lucrative export contracts, no longer continued to develop new ideas. There was also another reason why enthusiasm for this 'new art' cooled in subsequent years. In the beginning the best pieces of Art Nouveau glass were conceived as works of art. They were collected by a small circle of informed collectors who prized them for their uniqueness. Such artefacts required complicated skills and were unsuited for purposes of commercial mass production.

But the aftermath of the 1900 Exhibition makes one thing clear. Commercially speaking there was a growing demand for 'collectable' glass. Even though it was eventually mass-produced, Art Nouveau glass was always intended for the collector and was keenly collected at the time of its manufacture. As a result there was scope both for the middle-of-the-road collector and the most committed connoisseur.

The expensive *'Pièces Uniques'* bore inscriptions and dedications,

6 Contemporary tinted photograph of Gallé glass exhibited at the International Art Exhibition in Dresden in 1901. Gallé pieces were already considered *objets de vertue* by this date.

7 Poster by Georges de Feure.

many of them in celebration of the new century. Many were bought by museums, but their splendour and their messages were short lived. After being exhibited for a short period, they became unfashionable, were considered unworthy of display and were relegated to basement storerooms. After the First World War, Art Nouveau had fallen right out of favour and became the subject of ridicule and scorn and for several decades one

hardly dared mention the words. Several art critics had already dismissed it early on with the prediction that it would be choked to death by its own insatiable appetite for beauty. Emile Zola, the French novelist mockingly described it as the 'Lily' style and dismissed it out of hand, referring to it as a 'beautiful corpse'. The English painter and self-styled seeker of beauty and truth, Walter Crane, called it a disease or form of suffering.

The pursuit of beauty for its own sake, as embodied by Art Nouveau, returned to favour as a reaction against the obsessive and stark machine-age aesthetic of subsequent decades. Art Nouveau has been rediscovered with a vengeance and as a result there has sometimes been too much stress on the inferior aspects of this period of design which hardly merit the attention they are receiving. The collector today looks back on the 1960s with nostalgia. It was a time when Art Nouveau glass was sold at auctions more or less as a joke, provided, that is; that there was bidding at all for such lots. There was apparently an occasion, at an auction in Munich, when the auctioneer had to offer a free Gallé vase to anyone who would volunteer any bid whatsoever for an assorted Art Nouveau lot.

The Transition from Art Nouveau to Art Deco

Art Deco art glass was intended for a far wider market than the more esoteric pieces produced during the Art Nouveau period, although they both now command comparable prices. Good glass of the period seems to fall into two categories. On the one hand there are the best pieces of mass-produced glass distinguished for their excellent design and on the other hand the rare artist-signed pieces.

8 Contemporary photograph from the German art journal *Kunst und Dekoration* for 1904, showing the glass department of the Berlin gallery of decorative arts 'H. Hirschfeld', with vases and lamps (seen on a Majorelle display stand), being offered for sale.

Glass and Glass making

It is not known when man first learned to manufacture glass, and it is often thought to have been a chance discovery; it is possible that the substance was first noticed forming in volcanic lava. Pliny, the Roman historian, gives an account of the discovery of glass, which, though perhaps not historically accurate, seems plausible enough. According to him it was discovered when some Phoenician sailors with a cargo of nitrate were blown off course to a river estuary somewhere in Syria. Unable to find any stones with which to build a fire they used lumps of nitrate which, they found, melted and in the smouldering heat combined with the sand on the river bank to form transparent streams of a liquid substance hitherto unknown to man.

There is undoubtedly a grain of truth in this account, as scientific experiments have proved that a mixture of soda and silica can melt and fuse even in an open flame. The melting point of glass is somewhere between 1300°C and 1550°C. At this temperature glass is a molten mass, which in order to be workable is cooled to a temperature of 250°C. The handling of this hot substance at the furnace requires skilled craftsmanship and great experience. The glass-worker must always bear in mind the temperature of the glass, for it is this that determines its plasticity. This calls for a quick mind and keen alertness.

He knows he must begin and complete each separate process as quickly as possible, as the consistency of the material is controlled by its temperature. Consequently it is customary for glass to be re-heated repeatedly to a higher temperature during the process of manufacture. The most revolutionary development in glass-making was the introduction approximately 2000 years ago of the glass-blower's pipe. With its help the hot liquid substance could be blown into hollow shapes. This simple device consists of a steel pipe about 100-175cm long and approximately one centimetre in diameter. At one end there is a mouthpiece and a wooden (heat insulating) grip, and at the other end the tube widens out to a flat disc-like base. The flat end is dipped into the molten liquid prepared in a vessel inside the furnace. The molten liquid is a honey-like substance that sits on the end of the tube enabling the pipe to be rotated without the glass on the end of the pipe slipping, and the 'gather' of glass can then be shaped by 'marvering' or smoothing the gather on a rolling table with a surface of iron, copper, marble or lightly moistened wood. It is shaped by rolling into a roughly symmetrical shape. If in the meantime the 'gather' has cooled too much, it must again be held in the furnace and reheated to the required temperature; this can happen at any stage during production. The glass is now shaped into a hollow vessel. This is achieved either completely freehand by swinging, pulling and blowing, or by manipulating the material with simple tools, iron knives, shears and pincers.

Glass-blowing is a completely freehand technique, as contrasted with glass blown into a mould; when a mould is used the molten mass is blown into a detachable wooden or metal mould. The free-hand technique can be compared to the art of the potter throwing a pot on the wheel. Both potter and glass-blower rely in the same way on a rotating action and both require similar skills. An added complication for glass-blowers is that their substance is hot and can only be shaped with tools and not by hand. The glass-blower has another way of embellishing his work, and that is by adding coloured substances. In this event he has not only to concentrate on shape, but also on the varying behaviour pattern of each coloured glass substance. By clever rotations, re-heating and cooling processes the colours can combine to form artistic patterns. The art of applying trailing lines of colour has been practised from the earliest times. This process is one in which glass threads are spun on to the body of the vessel, and stand out in light relief after the cooling process has ended. A variation of this technique, and one which requires great skill, is for coloured threads to be inlaid in the glass, in such a way that they lie beneath the surface, and are seen through the body of the glass. The Venetians were the great masters of this particular art, and discovered a way of introducing a fine trellis effect in the glass, using different coloured threading.

During the Art Nouveau period the art of 'feathering' was one of the most notable innovations, this was the art of mixing various colours, and then with the help of a comb-like instrument, of making wavy patterns, somewhat reminiscent of the veining in leaves.

Another important technique in the history of Art Nouveau art glass was that of marquetry, a process where glass of various colours was cut while still hot and then inlaid into the body of the glass to form a pattern before cooling. This is not only a highly skilled art, but also one that involves a high element of

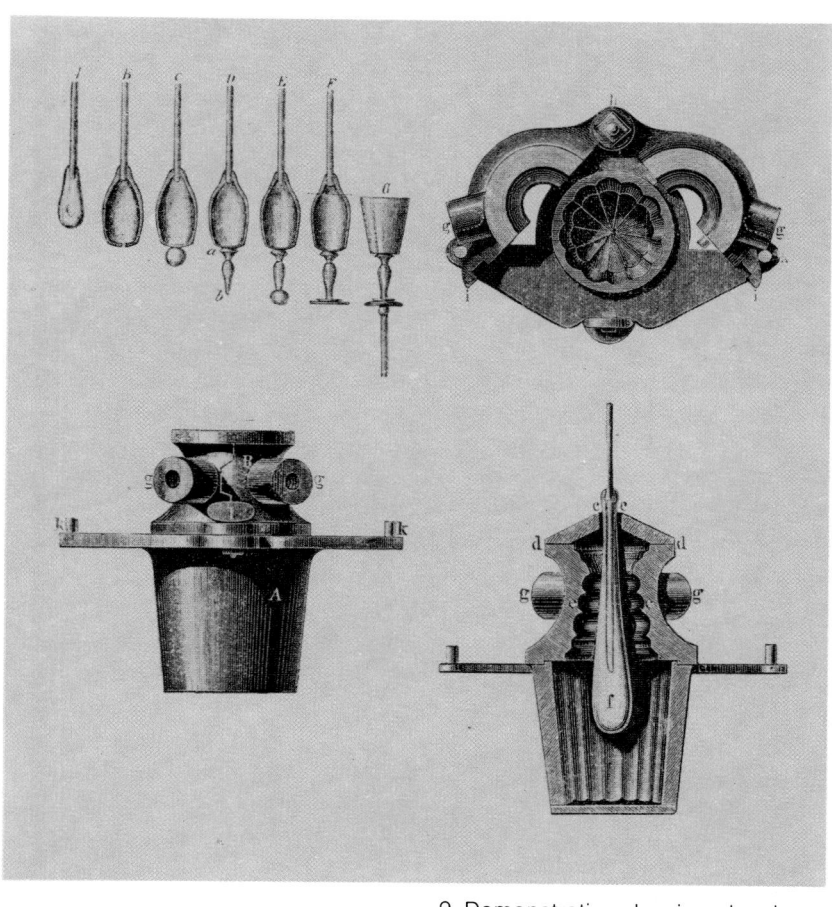

9 Demonstration drawing showing
equipment from a manual on
techniques of glass making.

risk. The reason for this element of
danger is that during the cooling
process the separate colours
undergo differing stresses, which
can result in the glass shattering.

This cooling (or 'annealing') process
has to be as carefully supervised
as that of the initial melting,
because it is during this process
that the actual patterns form.
The cooling is done in cooling-
ovens where the temperature is

carefully controlled, but it has to
be done quickly enough for the
glass not to become crackled or
form crystals. The 'annealing'
process is comparable to freezing,
in that the individual molecules do
not have time to form a protective
outer coating. Glass, although not
as resilient as a fluid, is tougher

than solid matter. Over the centuries craftsmen have got the process of finding the right chemical mixture down to a fine skill.

Their ideal had been to achieve crystal-clear transparency. For this reason they concentrated on finding the most suitable substance for a combination of clarity and durability.

The Venetians had the field to themselves well into the seventeenth century (where clear glass was concerned). Their glass is called soda-glass because of the high content of soda (derived from the ashes of plants). The great advantage of soda-glass was its malleability, but its drawback was its brittleness and the risk of its becoming cloudy if the proportion of soda was not calculated exactly. During the eighteenth century the supremacy of Venice was threatened by two countries; on the one hand the Bohemians made glass that was more durable, by using a mixture of sand, potash and chalk, that they had been developing since the beginning of the eighteenth century; at the same time the English developed lead-crystal glass, which was particularly suitable for the cut and engraved decoration which were then becoming fashionable, so fashionable in fact that the skill of the glass-cutter was beginning to be considered more important than that of the glass-blower.

Two important features of Glass

Glass makers of the period from 1890 to 1930 developed iridescent effects more closely related to metal than to glass substances. They also developed a technique of producing polychrome glass which resembled geological specimens more than conventional glass. Such iridescent surfaces were a complete change from the accepted traditions of crystalline transparency. It was the range of colour invented and used by Art Nouveau glass workers that was the most surprising innovation;

10 Pedal-driven grinding lathe with fixed grinder for glass-cutting.

apart from that there are two main styles of Art Nouveau glass. First of all there is the style developed by Tiffany, whose coloured glass can be instantly recognized, and whose main concern was to perfect the art of shaping by glass-blowing. By contrast other glass craftsmen attached more importance to carving or etching on the body of the glass. To them the blowing of glass shapes was of secondary importance, and took second place to the skill of sculpting the decoration.

Coloured Glass

Colour plays as important a role in art glass as it does in painting. The colours can be transparent or opaque, lightly tinted or solid. It is as difficult and complex to produce coloured glass as it is to produce the crystal clear variety. The spectrum is a wide one, ranging from colourless crystal to pitch black opaque lithalin glass.

Between these extremes there is an endless range of exciting possibilities with regard to colour. As it is possible to introduce colour into glass in varying degrees of intensity, any degree of opacity or transparency is attainable. Glass for instance can be either solid and opaque, or light and translucent. When layers of coloured glass are placed one upon another colour variations can be created as subtle

11 Pictures of the Gallé glassworks. The two top photographs show workers in the process of decorating and carving. This was the most laborious procedure involved in cameo-glass manufacture for even the industrial pieces had to be covered with various layers of acid-resistant varnish, and the process had to be repeated after each acid dipping. Polishing, grinding and enamel painting were also time consuming. It has been established that Gallé entered on cards the time taken to complete each individual piece so as to keep a close check on the efficiency of his schedule. The photograph at the bottom shows the actual glassworks, where the glass was melted and shaped. Three hundred workers were employed here, including blowers, designers and carvers.

as those attained by paint on canvas. The final colour depends on the colour and intensity of the separate layers, and the overall effect of their juxtaposition.

In chemical terms glass is coloured by the addition of metal oxides. These oxides are added either before or during the melting process; the addition of iron oxide produces a greenish colour, which turns to a yellower green with the addition of oxygen, and blue-green if more is added. Brownish colours can be achieved with iron-oxide, while copper-oxide produces greeny-blue, turquoise or even red. The addition of manganese oxide in small quantities reduces colour intensity, but when added in larger quantities it colours the glass purple, bordering on brown. An intense blue can be achieved by the addition of cobalt oxide.

Antimony gives a yellow colour, or, if added in greater proportion, opalescent white. Tin, uranium and chromium oxides are used for colours within the yellow to green spectrum. Milk or ivory glass is made by adding bone to the glass, and opalescence is achieved when bone is added in smallish quantities.

Iridescence

The colour and shading of Art Nouveau glass, though important, is not as vital as a lustre effect reminiscent of the iridescence of soap bubbles, or mother of pearl, or on the plumage of exotic birds. Again metallic oxides are used for these effects. Glass found in Roman archaeological digs has been much described. Such glass owes its iridescence to a thousand years of ageing. The glass has lain buried in the earth where its surface was corroded by contact with mineral salts.

This resulted in a shimmering iridescence much admired in the later part of the nineteenth century, and experiments began at that time to try and achieve similar effects with the use of chemicals. There were two ways of doing this: one way was to leave the glass in a solution of metallic salts; the other was to expose the cooling glass to metallic fumes. The earliest attempts at iridescence were exhibited at the Vienna World Fair, in the Hungarian section, where the glass manufacturer J.P. Zahn, exhibited crystal glass with rainbow effects. A few years later the traditionally conservative Viennese firm of J. & L. Lobmeyer began experimenting with iridescence. At this stage it left only a faint sort of soap-bubble effect on the surface of the glass. Louis Comfort Tiffany, in America, was bolder and artistically more adventurous with his experiments. By adding tin salts, strontium nitrate and barium nitrate, he achieved a far stronger iridescence, much to the amazement of the glass-collecting world. In Bohemia, glass makers followed suit and the company of Loetz Witwe under the directorship of Ritter von Spaun got techniques of iridescence up to a fine art. Like Louis Comfort Tiffany, the Loetz firm tried a wide range of chemical experiments. Interestingly enough, Loetz introduced iridescence at varying stages. Much Loetz glass has internal 'feathering' of a silvery colour, and the surface a separate shimmer of its own. This produces a complex iridescence, that has a brilliant metallic effect as light hits it.

The Art of Glass Cutting

The inspiration for Art Nouveau cameo glass is to be found in antiquity. From the earliest history of art glass there has been an

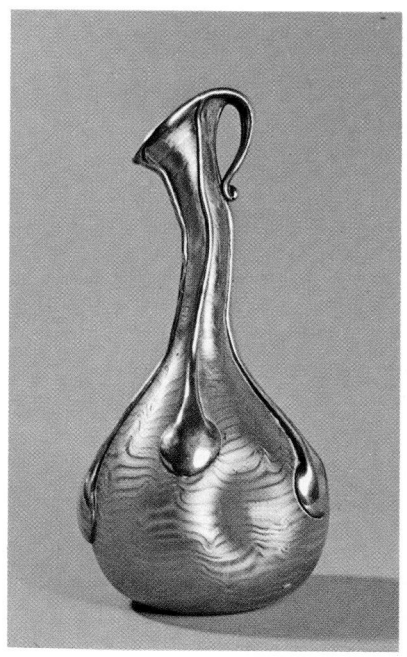

12 Loetz Vase; Bohemia. Height 23.5 cm, c. 1900. The shape is based on a Persian rosewater sprinkler. The vase is basically yellow, decorated with wavy silver lines worked into the glass whilst still hot. The elongated blue teardrop shapes were applied later.

13 Loetz Vase, Bohemia. Height 24.3 cm, c. 1900. Here too a stripy pattern was worked into the cobalt blue body of the glass in the early stages, before the vase assumed its final shape. The lower half of the vase is thinly covered with a silvery layer, which spreads upwards in irregular splashes.

14 John Northwood's copy of the Roman Portland Vase. The dark blue body of the vase is overlaid with opalescent white, and the decoration has been carved from this upper layer. Height 26.4 cm, 1876.

almost continuous tradition of carved glass. The techniques of intaglio carving on semi-precious stones were already far advanced in early times and these were simply transferred to glass. The most important milestone in the history of glass carving in the manner of ancient cameos is the Portland Vase, now in the British Museum. This is reputed to be the work of a Roman cameo worker of the first century A.D. The vase is amphora-shaped and has a thin layer of white glass over a cobalt blue ground. This white layer was further carved and cut to give an added depth of relief to the silhouette figures. This elegant and delicate art form was much admired in Victorian times, and discerning collectors spent great sums having copies of this masterpiece made for their own collections. In 1876, John Northwood, the English glass artist (1837-1902), won a prize of £1000 offered by the Stourbridge glass firm of Benjamin Richardson, for a perfect replica of the Portland Vase. This heralded a fashion in

England which stylistically never quite managed to shake off its classical antecedents. The art of glass carving developed along different lines in France; the French, inspired by the feat of the Portland Vase, gave expression to this art form in Art Nouveau terms. It was above all Emile Gallé, the famous glass craftsman and aesthete, who used classical and Oriental techniques to develop an expressive new European art form. Technically speaking, glass-carving is the most complex form of glass treatment. In marked contrast to Bohemian crystal cutting of the seventeenth and eighteenth centuries, which was merely a matter of cutting into a coloured surface, the art of cameo cutting developed by Art Nouveau glass artists was one of cutting separate layers of coloured glass. This process of cutting away layers with copper wires of differing thicknesses was both extremely laborious and very time-consuming, and for this reason specialised techniques of acid etching were developed in England and France to cut into the glass layers. Basically the effect was the same, but the acid process constituted a complete break with ancient techniques. For the collector of Art Nouveau glass however, there is a great difference both materially and aesthetically between hand carved and acid etched glass.

The particular innovation of Art Noveau cameo carving lay not in the techniques employed but in the designs chosen. Glass cutting had developed along traditional lines and had evolved rather gradually during the Eighteenth century and the earlier part of the Nineteenth century. There were no great surprises until Gallé made a complete break with tradition and evolved his deeply personal style; he even broke away from his own earlier style, as he started life as an imitator (chiefly of Persian-style glass) and it was not until the 1880s that he branched into Art Nouveau.

In some ways he remained a 'Victorian' in so far as his work was loosely based on Oriental designs and closely connected with the passion for 'Japonisme' during the 1870s and 1880s. But whereas the artists of the 'Aesthetic Movement' merely incorporated Oriental motifs into their designs, Gallé went further and was inspired to use them as the basis for a wholly European art-form.

16 Decorative glass vase with silver mount, possibly by Ernst Riegel. Darmstadt c. 1900; and a clear Bohemian glass goblet, with black enamel decoration after a design by the *Wiener Werkstatte* artist Dagobert Peche; manufactured by the *Wiener Werkstatte*, c. 1920. Dagobert Peche was a versatile designer who also did designs for furniture, lamps, silver, wall-hangings, book-jackets and textiles.

Art Nouveau Glass from Bohemia, Germany and Austria

At the turn of the century most of the glass available on the market came from Bohemia. Bohemia far superceded France in volume of production, although Bohemian glass of this period never achieved the same definition of style as French glass. The Bohemian glass industry was too diffuse and depended too greatly on export orders to achieve the same degree of fruitful collaboration between art and industry as in France.

National boundaries at the time we are speaking of make it impossible to consider Bohemia as a self-contained unit. It would be better to talk of a 'glass-producing area' including the province of Bohemia and the small states near to it. Until the First World War, Bohemia was a part of the Austro-Hungarian Empire, and, as such, was controlled by Austria, like the

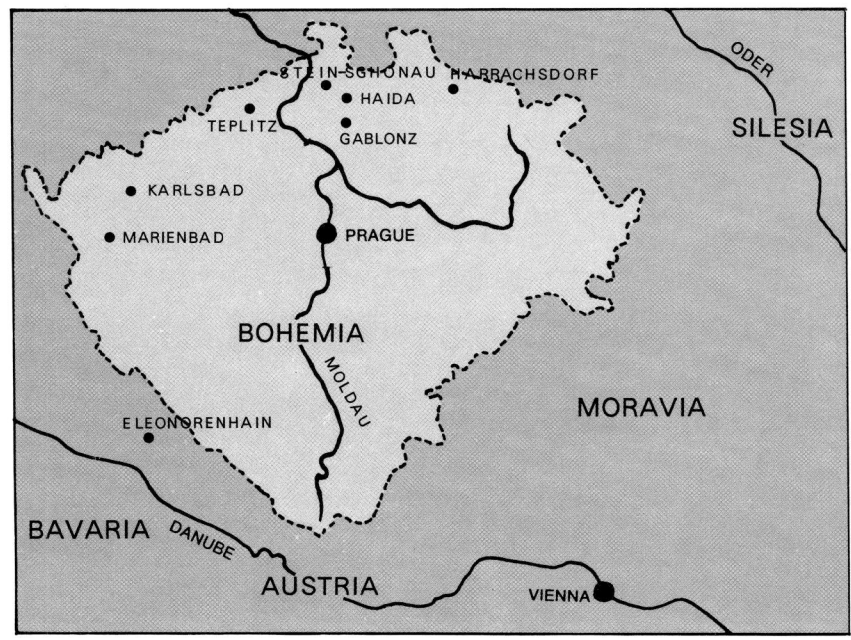

neighbouring states of Silesia, Thuringia and Bavaria. Together these areas constitute the oldest established and most productive manufacturing centre for traditional glassware in Central Europe.

Due to the wide variety of techniques and styles evolved during this period, every opportunity remains for forming a representative collection of Art Nouveau and Art Deco glass, without spending a fortune. As yet the price of good Bohemian glass of that period is not nearly as high as comparable French glass produced during the same period. This does not apply however in the case of Loetz glass.

A few facts and figures will suffice to determine the enormous scope of the Bohemian glass industry. During the 1920s there were 30,000 glass blowers working in Bohemia, and nearly 90,000 decorators busy engraving, cutting, painting and embellishing glass wares. The glass industry was concerned to a large extent with the manufacture of buttons, imitation pearls, and other glass accessories. Only a very small section of the glass industry was involved in the manufacture of decorative Art Nouveau glass. As always, they concentrated on traditional crystal cutting in Bohemia, and made drinking glasses and 'souvenir' ware for worldwide export.

The Traditional Firms

The most important of the Bohemian cut crystal firms was that of J. & L. Lobmeyr, the Viennese company founded in 1882. Like every successful Viennese industry, Lobmeyr farmed out part of its workload to companies in neighbouring provinces. Wilhelm Kralik's company soon became part of the Lobmeyr concern through inter-marriage; Kralik in turn owned the company of Meyrs Neffe. Apart from this Lobmeyr had already, early on in its history, acquired a company in nearby Marienthal as well as the rival Viennese firm of Janke and Gomer, and had leased a glass-works in Slovakia.

Such an empire was typical of the business traditions of the day, and under the directorship of Ludwig Lobmeyr, the company achieved a high standard of glass production. They produced traditional, middle-of-the-road Bohemian styles, and helped to consolidate the well-established Bohemian reputation for manufacturing the thinnest of thin glass in elegant shapes with the finest engraving and cutting. Lobmeyr adopted a Renaissance style which they first exhibited at the great International Exhibition of 1873 in Vienna. At the exhibition the Lobmeyr concern built their own pavilion and filled it

with the finest glass. It was an ambitious project for which they contracted the best glass cutters in the whole of Bohemia and aimed to produce glass which would be unique in quality. Famous artists designed and decorated bowls and chalices for them in the Renaissance tradition. Only when Lobmeyr's nephew took control of the company shortly after the turn of the century, did the company broaden its scope by including work done in a contemporary style. It was at this time that the architect Josef Hoffman came to do some stylish designs for Lobemyr, in which clear glass was decorated with delicate black or dark grey designs. This specialised technique, which can be used on opaque glass as well, is known as

17 The Exhibition Hall at the Vienna World Fair 1873, showing a display of glass exhibited by the firm of J. & L. Lobmeyr.

niello decoration.

It was the custom around 1900 for glass firms to commission the leading architects and designers of the day to design complete services for them. Peter Behrens, the famous German architect, designed a service for the Rheinische Glasshütten in 1901: it is severe in conception and has a red 'ruby-glass' design. Erich Kleinhempel, a designer and architect from Dresden, also worked for this firm. But designs by these artists only account for a very small percentage of the production of these firms. As always, the easiest glasses to sell were the German *Roemer*, or wineglasses with Renaissance garlands and all sorts of Neoclassical designs. If one looks through the catalogue of the Rheinische Glashütten, one sees old-fashioned patterns with names like 'Lohengrin', 'Clodwig', and 'Brunhilde'.

The Viennese Avant-Garde

It was against this background of conservative traditionalism that the Viennese avant-garde announced its revolutionary principles and began its experiments. Today the artefacts they produced are considered among the highlights of modern design.

The Viennese style is one for the connoisseur and in its own way compares favourably with the best in French design of the time. The layman could well ask why this Viennese style is rated so highly, as there is a distinct lack of the usual stylistic embellishments. Instead one finds a sophisticated stylishness, somewhat severe and cool in concept. The decoration is sparing and understated and the design based on principles of geometry and with great regard for the intrinsic qualities of the material itself. Metal mountings are studiedly simple, decoration often simply basic black and white, and it is in the very economy of these designs that their appeal lies.

Austrian glass designers did not think of decoration as an end in itself; they had a more modest approach than the French with their philosophy of 'art for art's sake', which claimed that design should always be practical as well as beautiful, so that an object could become a part of one's life in a practical sense as well. This was the Viennese contribution to Art Nouveau.

The founding of the *Wiener Werkstätte* in 1903 was to have the greatest possible influence on Viennese design in the decades to come. Under the directorship of the avant-garde designers Josef Hoffman (1870-1956) and Kolo Moser (1868-1918), the most creative Viennese artists and craftsmen came together to work as a corporate body, and produced artefacts of the greatest possible artistic merit. They took as their example the English Arts and Crafts Movement inspired by William Morris and his workshops. The manifesto of the *Wiener Werkstätte* stressed the problems of an artist/craftsman working in an industrial age bent on mass production. As the *Werkstätte* manifesto drawn up by Hoffman and Moser stated:

'An uncontrollable cancer has spread through the design world in the shape of, on the one hand, bad mass production, and on the other, imitations of obsolete styles masquerading as current art forms.

18 Art Nouveau vase in a gilt bronze mount. Metal mounts were popular during the Art Nouveau period. They were usually made of lead or zinc. This illustration however shows a bronze mount of exceptional design. It was designed by Gustav Gurschner who was famous for his figural Art Nouveau designs. The purple glass is by Loetz. The iridescence comes from shiny silver glass splinters incorporated into the main body of the glass. This type of glass was referred to by Loetz as 'Papillon' or 'Butterfly' glass, and was a novelty that attracted much attention. Height 27.7 cm, Austria c. 1900.

We have lost that feeling for art which our fathers had, and are tossed about on a thousand different currents. The machine has superceded the craftsman, and the businessman has replaced the artist. It would be folly to swim against this tide of events. It is for this reason that we have established the *Wiener Werkstätte*. On home ground, amid the roar of the machine, this will provide a haven of peace. We welcome those principles of workmanship proposed by Ruskin and William Morris. We appeal to all of you who feel it important to establish a cultural

encourage the most interesting modern trends in Vienna at the time. As early as 1880 this company had shown interest in the Vienna Secession movement. Bakalovitz also had the sole agency for Loetz who manufactured superb iridescent glass. The Vienna Secession reached its artistic peak around 1910, by which time Art Nouveau in France was on the decline, and had degenerated into copies and repetitions of established designs, often in the cheapest material. From the beginning the *Wiener Werkstätte* designers were important

19 Drinking glasses designed by Otto Prutscher for the Vienna glass firm of E. Bakalowits. The illustration comes from the German art journal *Deutsche Kunst und Dekoration, for* 1908.

figures in the art world, and even in the production of household goods, the hand of these designers is detectable. Although such artefacts are often unsigned, they are distinguished by a stylistic flair that was the Viennese trademark. The collector today has to rely on illustrations in contemporary journals to identify designers of such objects. He will in many cases

tradition of this kind and ask you to lend support to our aims and bear with mistakes we make along the way'.
The glass company of E. Bakalowitz took great pains to

have to be satisfied with a similarity of certain basic design characteristics, as only a small percentage of things designed at the time are actually to be found illustrated in such contemporary art journals as *Deutsche Kunst und Dekoration*. Plate 19 shows a photograph from a contemporary magazine of glasses designed by Otto Prutscher, and which can serve as a general stylistic guide, since the glasses have characteristics which distinguish them as unmistakably Viennese and serve in lieu of a Vienna Secession signature. The drinking glasses illustrated here have unusually long stems with square faceting which makes a decorative geometric design.

Loetz/Austria

Iridescent glass played an important role in the artistic development of Viennese and Bohemian glass. Both commercially and artistically speaking it was considered by Europeans as an alternative to the French carved or etched cameoglass. The new effects that Tiffany was striving for with painstaking experimentation, were achieved in Bohemia with no particular effort. In Bohemia they already had a head start of several decades, and had been experimenting with iridescent effects in coloured glass. Bohemian stone glassware had

been in production for a good fifteen years. This type of coloured, marbled glass looked like carved semi-precious stone. Bohemian coloured glass covered such a wide spectrum that it was technically

Marks of Loetz

possible to produce almost any colour. The firm of Johann Loetz Witwe situated in the small village of Klostermühlen in southern Bavaria established itself as the leading manufacturer of coloured glass within a very short space of time. The firm was founded in 1836 by Johann B. Eisner von Eisenstein, but was sold only four years later to the glass manufacturer Johann Loetz (1778-1848). After his death, his widow continued to run the firm, calling it Johann Loetz Witwe (the widow of Johann Loetz),. by which name the firm became known in subsequent years. When her son-in-law, Max Ritter von Spaun took over the firm in 1879, this small, out-of-the-way company started on a path of progress that soon caused it to become world famous. Spaun combined artistic ambition and administrative talent; such a combination of creative imagination

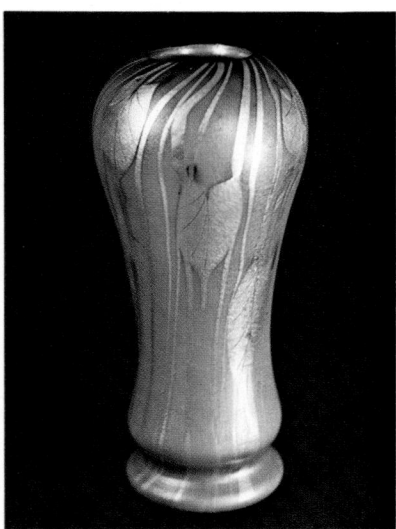

and administrative skill was a frequent formula for success during this period. The firm of Loetz, despite its remote location, took part in all international exhibitions, and received ever-increasing export orders. They soon had agents in most major cities. In Vienna, they were represented by the famous glass manufacturer E. Bakalowitz & Sons, in Paris by Salon Diespeke, in Hamburg by Ernst Codes, in Berlin by Lug Frankel, and in London by F. Crasa & Co. The next step came when Loetz put on a display of their most recent achievements at the Industrial Fair

20 Loetz vase. Baluster form vase with four applied handles; with engraved signature on the base 'Loetz, Austria'. The iridescence comes from glass splinters melted into the body of the glass, ('Butterfly decoration'). Height 24.9 cm, Bohemia c. 1900.

21 Spherical Loetz vase, with blister like applications and gold iridescence. Height 12.3 cm, after 1900.

22 Loetz vase. Yellow brown glass with outer casing of green; inlaid with silver-gold leaf and bud design. Both shape and decoration are reminiscent of Tiffany. Height 23.9 cm, Bohemia c. 1900.

23 Vases all signed 'Loetz/Austria'. *From left to right.* Vase with three openings in honey-coloured glass with silvery blue lustre. Height 16.5 cm. Four-handled wine-red vase, with greeny-gold lustre and 'oil spot' decoration. Height 29.4 cm. Milky yellow glass with applied decoration. Height 12.6 cm. All vases date from 1900.

in Munich. Loetz won a prize for various inventions such as 'onyx-glass' (a substance imitating brownish coloured stone), or 'Cornelia' (a reddish glass substance), 'Intarsia' (glass with coloured chasing over a clear base), and 'Octopus', (a dark blue glass with applied gold decoration.
In 1893 Loetz exhibited their 'Columbia glass' at the World Fair in Chicago. This glass had a strong iridescent surface with small applied medallions showing the face of Christopher Columbus. Also on show were *'Pavonia'* and *'Persika'* ranges of glass; they were both coloured glass with interesting iridescent effects. There was also so-called 'Alpine red' and 'Alpine green' glass as well as 'Camelia red'.
In 1900 at the Paris World Fair they widened their palette of colours and their range of shapes. The catalogue gives details of colour variations; for instance the *'Papillon'* ('Butterfly') design came in red, gold or blue, and had a shimmering iridescent effect which resembled butterfly wings. Then there was *'Phanomen'* ('Phenomenon'), where the body of the glass included wavy lines of different coloured glass threading, and there were other ranges such as 'Iris', 'Calliope', 'Cytius', 'Formosa' and 'Orpheus'.
This varied range of iridescent glass was intended to compete with

Tiffany glass. Loetz glass was made particularly attractive by being much cheaper to buy. At auction today certain combinations of colour and shape in Loetz glass can command prices as high as those fetched by Tiffany. There is still, however, no comprehensive monograph on Loetz, and so a collector has to use his own judgement in appraising and classifying a piece of Loetz glass. There are various distinguishing criteria for evaluating Loetz glass. A distinction should be made for instance between wavy banks of decoration, molten glass splinters pressed into the surface of the glass, overlaid tear drop shapes, feathering in the glass, and plain iridescent surfaces.
The shapes are no less important; many are inspired by forms from antiquity. Some have applied handles, others have asymetrical dimpled depressions, some imitate antique glass that has been corroded and weathered by age and some are bottle-shaped with irregular elongated necks similar to Persian rosewater sprinklers. Signatures on Loetz glass are insignificant, as unlike those on Gallé glass they are not part of the design. The only reason why Loetz glass was signed was to satisfy import regulations required by those countries to which Loetz exported its glass. For instance, United States regulations stated

24 Bohemian cut glass vases and bowls.

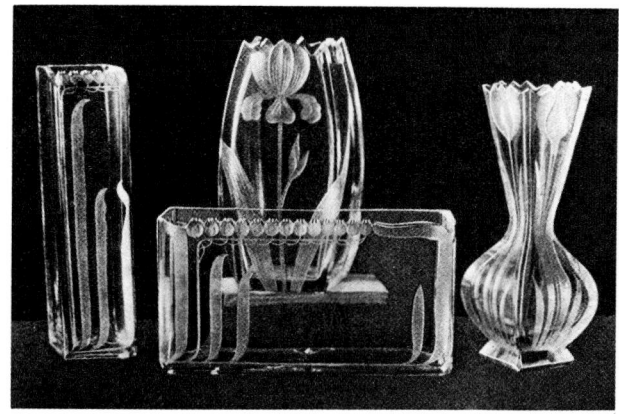

25 Iridescent vases with silver overlay decoration by Adolf Zasche, Gablonz 1901.

26 Faceted vases in marbled green and red 'Diluviam' glass by Josef Rindskopfs & Son in Kosten, Bohemia c. 1900

27/28 Examples of applied threading. This technique was widely practised in Bohemia; the glass threads were applied as the vase was cooling and already in its final shape, and not melted into the body of the glass whilst still hot.

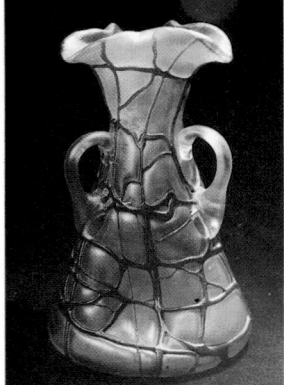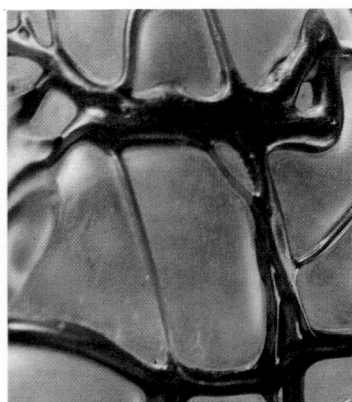

29/30 Examples of 'Papillon' decoration. The vase started off being funnel shaped, and was then pinched at the top in four places with pincers to make five openings.

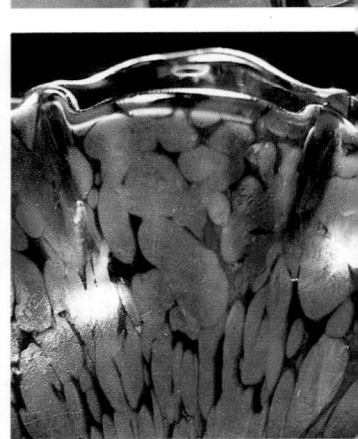

31/32 'Phäno-men' glass was made by incorporating wavy green internal decoration into yellow-bodied glass. Silver glass splinters were then pressed into the hot surface, which took on elongated oval shapes.

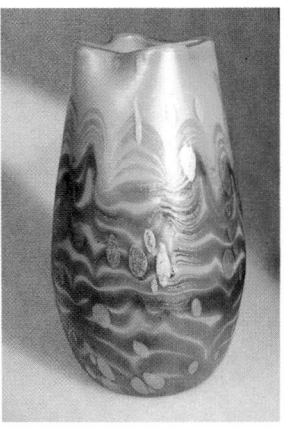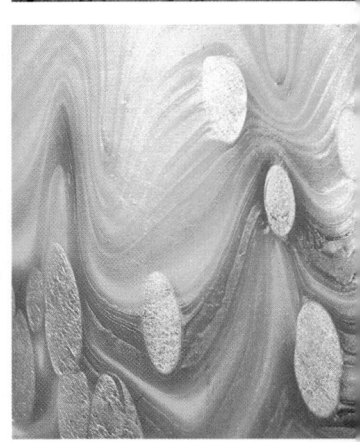

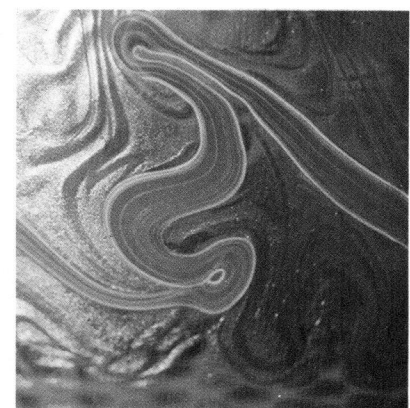

33-36 Loetz vase. The technical brilliance of this vase is ample proof of the highly developed skill of Bohemian glass manufacturers. The body of the glass has a pale opalescence, like Venetian 'lattice-work' glass, and like Venetian glass has a web of threads woven into it. The opalescent background is then inlaid with a wavy silver pattern, and a single rust-coloured decorative band. The overall effect is one of complete smoothness, despite the many colours used in the composition of the vase. The base of the vase is signed 'Loetz/Austria', which was the usual signature on vases intended for export. The illustration bottom right shows the same technique using a different colour scheme. The vase is also 13.3 cm in height and bears the same signature; it demonstrates how a basic pattern can be made in varying colours. Instead of a blue lattice background, the lattice-work is yellow here. The designer has however expressed himself freely in the random frieze of green decoration. Height 13.3 cm, Bohemia 1900.

37 Vases with enamelled decoration, made by Heckert of Petersdorf after designs by Sütterlin.

38 Vases by Carl Goldberg of Haida. Iridescent blue with etched silver decoration. (Contemporary photographs).

were often designed specifically to accompany a particular model. Often, too, the glass is overlaid with a design in strips of hand-wrought silver in Art Nouveau motifs, which has been pressed on to the glass. Figural mountings by sculptors are extremely rare. There are however, known to be some mounts by the sculptor Gustav Gurschner, some by the famous designer Kolo Moser, and there are some by Rudolf Bakalowitz, but only in very rare cases are any of these mounts signed. However the fact that they were designed is proof of the close relationship between glass manufacturers and the progressive Viennese design school. As only export models were signed, and many signatures found on Loetz glass are later additions, it requires experience or comparison with a known piece to establish authenticity. Also one must remember that Loetz encountered strong competition from manufacturers in neighbouring regions of Bohemia who tried to cash in on their success by producing very similar wares. It also often happened that glass designed by Bakalowitz was contracted out to be produced both by Loetz and Meyrs Neffe. The list of glass manufacturers producing iridescent glass in the style of Loetz is endless, and there are as many names to choose from as there are types of glass; trade

that imported glass be signed by the manufacturer and marked with the country of origin. For this reason many vases are signed with the etched 'Loetz/Austria' signature. Some vases show a pair of crossed arrows within a circle (the Loetz trademark), as well as the word 'Austria'. Only a few pieces have artists' monograms, but a signature is never an indication of quality. There are many Loetz vases with metal mounts. Such mounts are integral to the original pieces, and

39 A selection of Art Nouveau style wine glasses.

names like *'Persia'*, *'Semiramis'* and *'Alhambra'* are to be associated with the Rindskopf glassworks in Teplitz, *'Aspasia'* with the region of Schleiersee, *'Chameleon'*, *'Rhaptophan'*, *'Telama'*, *'Pettalon'*, *'Hekla'* and *'Corde'* with Frauenau, *'Helios'* with Eleonerenhain, *'Maja'* and *'Harka'* with the Ferdinand von Poschinger glassworks in Buchenau, and finally *'Marmopal'* with the Fritz Heckert glassworks in Petersdorf (Silesia).

If it is complicated to distinguish between the various Loetz types, it is almost impossible to distinguish between the firms listed above, even for the specialist, and he must rely completely on conjecture or his own experience in order to make attributions to any individual factory or designer.

There are three general rules which apply in identifying Loetz shapes.

1) Shapes based upon designs found in antiquity.

2) Pieces influenced by the linear designs of the *Weiner Werkstätte.*

3) Typical Art Nouveau shapes inspired by successful foreign designers.

The firm of Pallme-König &

40 Bohemian lidded jar from Steinschönau or Haida, with enamelled decoration.

41 Bohemian covered goblet and two bowls, c. 1925. Clear glass with gilding and painted enamel decoration; parts of the clear glass are tinted yellow. Height of the goblet 38 cm.

Habel in Steinschonau (with a subsidiary in Kosten in north Bavaria) was one of the many that owed a measure of their success to the precedent set by Loetz; this firm used ideas which Loetz had already proved to be successful. It employed a staff of 300, and, in addition to producing cut crystal, made iridescent glass and vases overlaid with a net-like web of spun glass threads (see plate 27). Perhaps the most remarkable

model they produced was a flower-form vase 30 centimetres high, in the style of Tiffany's Jack-in-the-Pulpit Vase. The attraction of these pieces lay in the fact that they cost a fraction of those they were copying.

The firm of Ludwig Moser in Bavaria, with a work force of 400, produced large quantities of glass. The glass most associated with the name of Moser is thick amethyst-coloured glass with a gilded frieze contained in a band near the rim, into which are etched classical figures. But Moser was a prolific firm and produced many styles of glass including some beautifully carved cameo glass. As a rule there is a layer of coloured glass over a transparent body and both layers are skilfully carved. The carving on this glass is extremely deep and glass of this sort is very rare. The firm (founded in 1857) was known for its high standard as much as for the fact that its designers included artists who worked for the *Wiener Werkstätte*. Among those who designed for the firm were Josef Hoffman, Hilde Jesser, J. Wimmer and also Dagobert Peche.

The Moser glass factory produced an extraordinary variety of pieces. The heavier pieces are often signed, 'Moser Karlsbad'. Another important name in the field of mass-produced glass was Carl Goldberg in Haida, a self-made man who started the business in 1881.

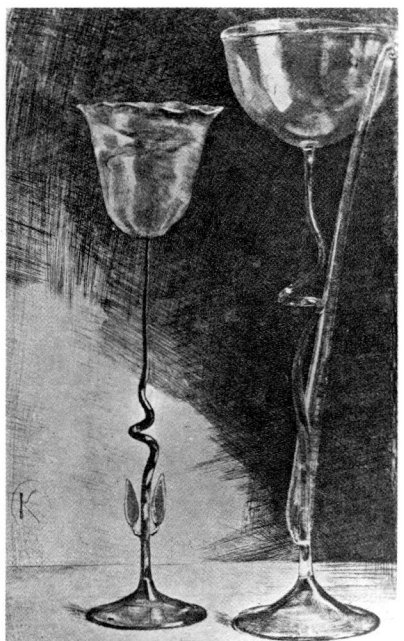

42 Etching by Karl Koepping from the decorative art magazine *Pan*, used by him as a model for his glasses.

He employed 200 people and within a short while was producing gold-rimmed, cut crystal as well as engraved drinking glasses, Art Nouveau vases with enamelled decoration, etched glass vases with brilliant silvered decoration, and also French style cameo glass decorated with floral designs and with a prominent signature. Carl Goldberg was responsible for inventing a type of enamelled decoration which consisted of applying enamel colours in relief onto the surface of the glass.

This technique could be made to look like cameo glass, but the process was far simpler and cheaper.

Famous outsiders: Koepping and Zitzmann

Glass need not neccessarily be made in a factory; it can be shaped without a furnace, and embellished in a studio by engraving, cutting or acid etching; it can in fact be shaped just as well at home in front of an open flame. For such work, glass tubes or hollow glass piping of 2 centimetres diameter are used, and this can be pulled and shaped in the heat. This is a technique that had been used for centuries. In Thuringia and Bohemia there was a thriving cottage industry for the manufacture of Christmas tree decorations, toys, tiny glasses for dolls' houses and above all for glass beads.

There were also so-called travelling 'glass spinners' who practised their art at festivals and fairs. In Murano it is still customary today to blow glass vases and little figurines in front of an open flame.

Signature of Karl Koepping

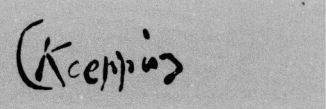

One of the few artists who practised this technique during the Art Nouveau Period, was Karl Koepping, born in Dresden in 1848. He studied to be a painter, engraver and chemist, and after a long stay in Paris during the 1890s was summoned to Berlin to take up a post as professor of engraving and graphics. Here he made engravings which were in fact designs for glass and were published in the discerning art journal 'Pan' which he helped to edit. His glass was paper thin; from the finely modelled base there rose a fragile plant-like stem with curling blade-shaped, pointed leaves, and a fine cup shaped like a bud. Koepping allowed Friedrich Zitzmann (1840-1906) to copy his glass designs. Zitzmann was famous for his ability to make exact copies of Seventeenth-century Venetian wine glasses in front of an open flame. He had demonstrated his art on numerous occasions before the many 'Societies of Arts and Crafts' which had at that time become so popular in Germany. But Zitzmann only executed Koepping's earliest designs, as after a short while Zitzmann began producing pieces of glass under his own name in Wiesbaden which were close copies of Koepping's work.

After they parted company Koepping had his designs executed in Ilmenau (in Thuringia) at the 'Grand Ducal Saxon School of Arts and Crafts and College for Glass Instrument Makers and Glass Technicians'. From this time on it is not surprising that the designs were patented and were prominently signed 'Koepping'.

Thanks to the patronage of the Paris art dealer, Samuel Bing, Koepping's glass received international publicity and became world famous. Bing presented these glasses for sale in specially designed silk lined boxes with a gold printed inscription. Today Koepping glass is worth a small fortune and as a result the market has been flooded with fakes, but as Zitzmann found out, Koepping's designs are not easy to copy.

W.M.F. Glass

The Wurttembergische Metallwarenfabrik in Geislingen near Stuttgart was known at the turn of the century for its well designed products including Art Nouveau glass with metal mountings. From 1883 a sister company was started in Göppingen for the manufacture of glass. But it was not until the 1920s that this company managed to evolve a style of its own. In 1921 a brand of glass known as 'Ikora Crystal' appeared on the market (see plate 45). It was produced cheaply, and made in great quantities and intended for the mass market.

The line met with great success. 'Ikora' included decorative bowls and vases made of thick glass with marblized streaks of red, violet, green and yellow. It is often found in antique shops today and is still inexpensive; it is never signed. In 1925 W.M.F. patented a new range of glass called 'Myra Crystal'. This is essentially a lightweight, greeny yellow glass with a golden finish which gives the glass a blue, green, purple or red iridescence. There is a silver base to this gold, which is what provides the iridescence; this was the discovery of the glass technician Karl Wiedmann (born 1905). The pattern book for 1926/27 lists 150 models of 'Myra' glass.

43 Bohemian and German Liqueur glasses from the 1920s, with bowls and stems of different colours.

44 'Myra' crystal bowl by WMF (*Wurttembergische Metallwaren - Fabrik*), with bluish gold iridescence. Germany *c.* 1930.

45 Various vases and bowls by WMF (*Wurttembergische Metall-waren - Fabrik*). This style of glass (known by the brand name 'Ikora') was mass-produced in Germany from 1921 to 1930.

46 Wine glasses by (*from right to left* Reichenbach (*the first two*), Moser, Powell and Christiansen.

47 A selection of typical 1920s glass. *From right to left*: Faceted Bohemian green glass box; wine-glass (probably Belgian) with black base; cut glass decanter and glasses; blue glass sweetmeat dish by Fachschule Zwiesel, 1925.

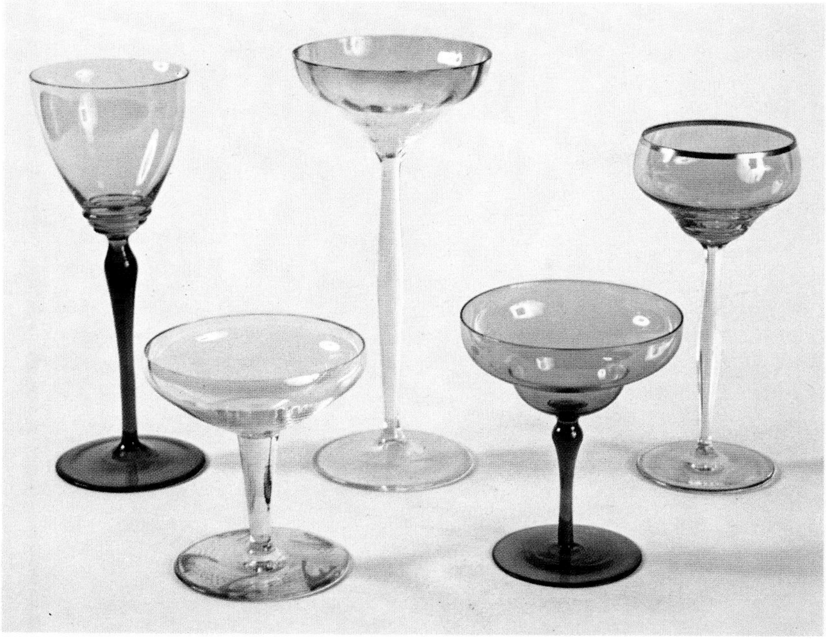

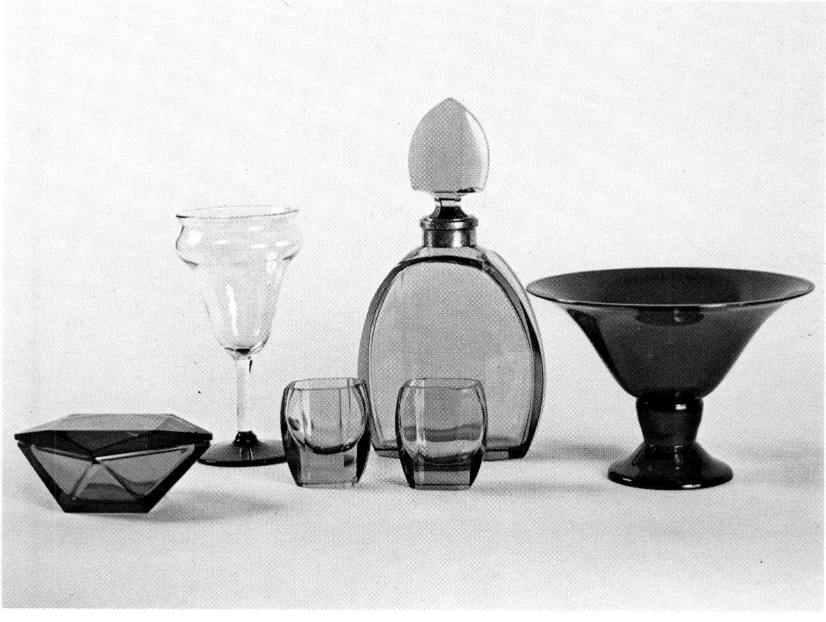

Art Nouveau in Belgium Holland and Scandinavia

There were a number of old-established glass firms all over Europe, not all of which got swept into the Art Nouveau movement. Val St. Lambert, Leerdam and the Swedish firm of Orrefors, in particular are of interest as glass by these firms is often to be found in antique shops or at auction.

Val St. Lambert

Val St. Lambert was a well equipped, modern factory, which, at the turn of the century employed 4500 workers, although

Signature of Val St. Lambert

little attention was paid to the manufacture of Art Nouveau glass there. This was remedied when the company eventually established contact with the famous Art Nouveau designers working in Brussels. Depres, the director of

Val St. Lambert at the time, commissioned the Art Nouveau architect Victor Horta to build a special pavilion for Val St. Lambert for the 1897 Brussels World Fair. Plate 48 shows one of the series of Val St. Lambert vases whose decoration was inspired by the abstract linear designs of Van de Velde; the technique used is a slight variation on the usual cameo technique in that the decoration does not appear in relief, but is carved in such a way that the linear design is on the sunken under layer and is revealed by carving the upper layer in depth. Apart from the vases, Val St. Lambert produced a number of pieces in the *'Ecole de Nancy'* style, with multi-coloured etched and carved floral decoration (for which the term *'fluorogravure'* was invented). One of the chief designers was the Paris trained artist Louis Léon Ledru, who worked as a designer for Val St. Lambert for 38 years. A catalogue dating from 1906/7 lists 411 different vases described as *'Articles genre Daum decorées par les frères Muller (Graveurs Acide)'* (Pieces in the style of Daum by the Muller brothers (acid-etchers). The brothers Henri and

48 Belgian Val St. Lambert cameo glass vases. In these vases the layer of coloured glass, over a clear base, is carved to provide the design.

Desiré Muller came from Croismaire but had been commissioned by Val St. Lambert to work for them for one year. The vases designed by them are distinctive because of their delicate colouring. They used separate layers of rusty red, shimmering violet, Indian yellow and reddish grey in their cameo glass, and then added enamel painted decoration. All the vases are signed VSL in etched relief.

Leerdam

The Royal Dutch Glassworks near Rotterdam were founded in 1765. They broke with the established tradition shortly before the First World War, when P.M. Cocius, the

Director at the time, commissioned the architect K.P.C. de Bazel (1869-1923) and the designer C. de Lorm (1875-1942) to work for them. The designs were executed in a shiny, lightweight, transparent glass which gave ample opportunity for decoration. These were attractive designs which would have a wide appeal and during the 1920s H.B. Berlage (1856-1934) continued this tradition.

In 1923 the company started a studio department and began their series of 'Serica' and 'Unica' vases. The 'Serica' pieces were put out in

limited editions. 'Unica' pieces were, as the name suggests, unique and signed accordingly. 'Unica' vases are signed in diamond point and the words 'Leerdam Unica' are followed by the name of the designer, a serial number and a letter denoting the year of manufacture.

Orrefors and Kosta

From 1897 onwards the Swedes were producing cameo glass with carved and acid-etched floral and landscape decoration in the style of Gallé. Swedish cameo glass artists include Gunner Gunnarson Vennerberg, Alf Wallander and Karl Lindeberg.

The glass made by Kosta and Orrefors (Orrefors Bruks Aktiebolag) is more interesting. The firm was founded in 1898 and produced glass in various colours including brown, topaz, amber and pale blue. Orrefors manufactured household glass, and developed a technique known as *graal-glass* which derived its inspiration from the work of Gallé. Another Orrefors speciality was engraved crystal, some of which is of truly outstanding quality.

---

49 Val St. Lambert cameo glass vase with orchids. Signed 'VSL'. Height 41 cm.

50 Leerdam drinking glass from a set by de Lorm. Leerdam, 1917.

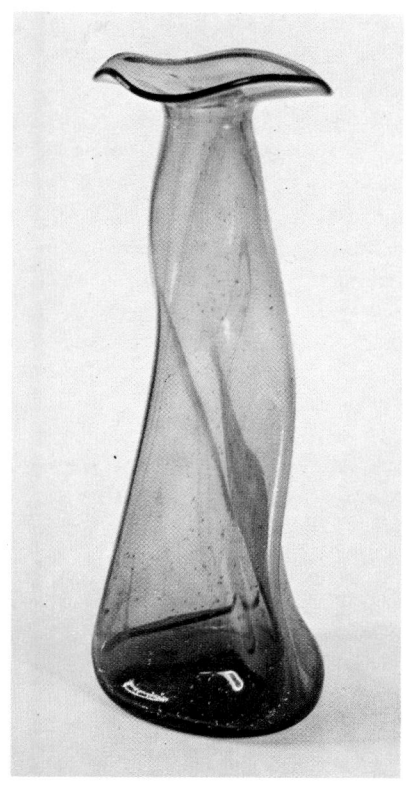

Art Nouveau in England

The Art Nouveau movement had strong British connections and in particular the so-called founding fathers of the Art Nouveau movement Ruskin and William Morris. The glass industry in England was a flourishing one and both technically and stylistically advanced.

Cameo Glass

French and English cameo glass techniques were similar, involving a process of working on the separate layers of glass. English cameo glass usually had a dark ground with a white cameo-cut relief design. The

51 Clutha glass, after a design by Christopher Dresser, stamped 'Clutha'. Glasgow, c. 1900.

52 Three-layered cameo glass with gilding by Thomas Webb & Sons. Height 18 cm.

white is carved more deeply in some places than in others, and the underneath colour shines through with different degrees of intensity determined by the various thicknesses of the top layer. The subtlest colour effects can be achieved by using this technique. Despite the fact that there are only two basic colours in the glass, the degrees of light and shade can be endless, and the overall effect is often surprisingly lifelike. The background colour of these pieces is usually either red or blue.

The model for this kind of glass, both for the French and the English, was the Portland Vase in the British Museum. Plate 14 shows John Northwood's copy of this famous vase. Some amazing pieces were executed in this style during the 1880s, based on classical models, as their titles suggest: 'Venus rising from the Sea', or 'Hercules restoring Alcestis to her husband Admetus'. Apart from this neo-classical style, there were hunting scenes, landscapes and flimsily draped female figures in the Pre-Raphaelite manner. Such cameo glass only became a commercial proposition when the decoration was acid-etched and not hand-carved. Thomas Webb and Son achieved renown for glass executed in this manner; they had earlier received acclaim for the work of the famous glass worker John Northwood (1837-1902) who spent years working on his amazing Pegasus Vase. Webb began to produce cameo glass commercially during the 1880s but did not use Art Nouveau motifs. They made vases, scent bottles and bowls, decorated with blossom, lilies, dragons, moorish motifs or female figures. These pieces were usually two-layer cameo glass, basically red or blue, with the decoration carved into the upper layer of ivory coloured glass.

The brothers George and Thomas Woodall are two of the best known English cameo glass artists. Stevens and Williams also produced cameo glass including pieces designed by John Northwood, who amalgamated his own studio with the larger, parent company in 1884.

Intaglio, Moss Agate, Silveria

Stevens and Williams was also famous for a kind of glass known as 'Moss Agate', which resembled the art glass manufactured by the French company Rousseau-Léveillé and involved a similar technique. The glass is heavily crackled and has oxide inclusions. Technically speaking it was soda-glass inlaid with powdered colour or with foil inclusions and cased with a layer of clear lead glass. This substance was dipped in water for a short while, until light crackling occurred

in the more brittle soda-glass. The
technique was further developed
by the American Steuben glassworks after Frederick Carder, the
artistic director of Stevens and
Williams, emigrated there in 1902.
With intaglio glass the carved
decoration does not stand out in
relief; it is, on the contrary, a
process of carving or cutting in
depth. Cameo and intaglio glass
bear a superficial resemblance to
one another but they are, in fact,
reverse processes.

In about 1900 John Northwood II
developed Silveria glass; this was a
technique known in Bohemia and
in France, where a combination of
clear and lightly coloured glass was
inlaid with metal foil and then
covered with a transparent layer.
This involved a highly complicated
technique, and manufacturing this
type of glass was a laborious
process.

Another technique used in English
glass-making, was 'threaded' glass.
This effect was achieved by using
specially designed machines which
could apply the threads evenly; a
comb-like appliance pulled the

53 A Stevens and Williams Moss
Agate vase of crackled pale amber
with dark inclusions. Height 14 cm,
c.1900.

54 A selection of wine glasses by
James Powell & Son, c.1900.

55 A Webb carved glass jug with
elaborate floral and figurative
motifs, c.1880.

threads through the glass to give it a 'feathered' look similar to the 'combed' or 'feathered' effect of Loetz glass.

The firm of James Powell & Son made vases which were distinguished for their simple but beautiful shapes. Apart from making stained glass windows, they also produced drinking glasses of unusually fine quality. These have become popular collectors' items, and are remarkable for their simple elegance and stylistic assurance.

Clutha Glass

Glass produced under the tradename 'Clutha' by the Glasgow firm of James Couper & Son was more avant-garde in style, and closer to the ideals of Art Nouveau. The glass was produced by rolling lightly coloured glass in coloured splinters and shimmering metallic particles as it was being shaped. The glass was then re-heated and worked into its final shape. It was produced in various shades of green and pinky-red (see plate 52) and occasionally in black. The texture of the glass is reminiscent of antique German 'forest glass' in which the final effect was also achieved by a sort of 'soiling' of the glass, which is what gave the glass its appealing visual effect. It is from this 'muddy' look that the glass derives its name, 'Clutha' being old Gaelic for cloudy.

It is not only the texture of the glass but the shapes too that have a medieval feel to them. The pieces were first free blown and then pinched and twisted to give them their final shape, as with Tiffany and Loetz glass. These organic shapes found a ready market and made a welcome change from run-of-the mill, commercially produced Victorian glass. Liberty & Co. took on the agency for Clutha glass. Designers such as George Walton (1867-1933) worked for Clutha, and also Christopher Dresser (1834-1904), whose overall genius as a designer and craftsman led him to produce designs for cast iron, silver, furniture, textiles and glass. Clutha glass is not always signed, but easily recognisable. When it is signed, the name 'Clutha' is written in full in a semi-circle around a floral emblem. The pieces designed by Dresser bear the initials 'C.D.' in addition.

56 Tiffany flower-form vases. The fragility of these pieces is reminiscent of Venetian glass. The vase on the left is made of yellowish glass, with gold iridescence, and the attached foot is of reddish-blue glass. The middle vase is a yellow honey-colour, mixed with milky yellow, and incorporates an abstract plant-form design. The vase on the right has a green stem, and a white bowl, iridescent gold on the inside, and applied green feathering outside. Heights 27.2 cm, 44 cm and 33.5 cm, New York c. 1900.

Art Nouveau in America

Tiffany Glass

Tiffany glass stands in a class by itself among American art glass of the period. One has only to look at other American glass made at the time to appreciate the superior quality of Tiffany's pinkish opalescent glass shot through with a peach-coloured iridescence. Tiffany was not interested in applied decoration of any sort; he was dismissive of the art of glass-cutting and of painted decoration. He was interested in pureness of design, and maintained that artistry in glass was a matter of the glass blower's skill at the furnace. Decoration as far as he was concerned was the result of technical skill in shaping and forming a piece of glass; the glass should assume its final form during the process of handling in the heat of the furnace; no decoration was to be applied once the glass had cooled. As a result the aesthetics of Tiffany art glass depend on the substance itself and the handling of it; it is never a question of any decorative skills except those involving the handling of glass at the furnace. For Tiffany decorating glass meant quite simply under-standing and exploiting its intrinsic properties. Under his own super-vision, Tiffany's workers were trained to practise the necessary skills for producing hand-crafted glass worthy of his name; Tiffany

glass is comparable from an aesthetic and a technical point of view to the Venetian masterpieces of the sixteenth and seventeenth centuries. The story of the Tiffany glassworks is typically American. Charles Lewis Tiffany (1812-1903), age twenty-five, left the family firm in the provinces, and with 1000 dollars in his pocket set off for New York. There, together with a college friend, he started the company of Tiffany and Young which began by importing jewellery from Italy, France and England. In 1850 Tiffany started producing his own brand of silver, which was of a fairly high standard, and a high enough grade of silver to be stamped 'sterling'. Soon he began importing and dealing in clocks, bronzes, jewellery and high quality decorative objects. In 1850 the firm managed to acquire a collection of diamonds once in the possession of Marie Antoinette, and in 1887 their financial position allowed them to purchase a large proportion of the French crown jewels that came on to the market at a price of 2,000,000 French francs. A little later they acquired the largest yellow diamond ever mined. Meanwhile Tiffany's company achieved world-wide renown with impressive branches in Paris and London. He won gold medals at all the important international fairs. In 1878 Charles Lewis Tiffany received the French

Légion d'Honneur.

His son, Louis Comfort Tiffany, was born in 1848. As he was financially independent, he decided to pursue artistic studies, and studied painting in the New York studio of the famous landscape artist George Innes. Innes is basically an 'American' painter, with a colour palette a little too bold for European tastes, and with a symbolist element in his work. But he was a good teacher, particularly of technique and composition. Tiffany also met with the artist Léon Bailly in Paris, who had a penchant for 'Orientalism' which was so fashionable at the time. It was his influence that caused Tiffany to travel to North Africa, Spain and Egypt. These journeys must have had a formative influence on his imagination. In 1892 Tiffany founded his first company, which he called The Tiffany Glass and Decorating Company. Other companies were to follow, as Tiffany developed various practical uses for art glass. He was already known for his stained glass windows, as well as for monumental mosaic paintings made up of small brilliantly coloured pieces of glass. For this work he required a large, skilled work force, capable of producing glass of all shapes and textures, capable of mounting stained glass in windows, and of making mosaic pictures. He employed a number of

57 **Louis Comfort Tiffany** (1848-1933).

chemists and glass experts to help him with these monumental creations. In his work he used a widely varied colour palette; his technique also depended on glass of varying textures some of them constructed to let the light through, and others opaque. The surfaces were composed of wave-like patterns, and the colour effects often achieved by superimposing or fusing colours. Apart from this already complex business operation, Tiffany started up a studio for the manufacture of decorative glassware. In 1893 he founded his first successful studio workshop at Corona (Long Island), where

antique shapes were copied in blown glass worked at the furnace. Eventually, following on the success of his early efforts, he opened as many as five other studios.

His glassworks were run on idealistic principles. He always encouraged his workers and generously allowed them to develop their own creative abilities. He sent his glass blowers on study tours, and gave them access to his own comprehensive collection of Islamic, Roman, Venetian and old German glass.

58 'Cypriote' Tiffany vase. 'Antiqued' glass on a bronze base. Signed 'K 1379'. Height 28 cm, c. 1900.

59 Tiffany peacock-eye vase. Height 30 cm. c. 1900.

60 Tiffany flower-form vase, signed 'L.C.T. - T. 290'. Height 17 cm, c. 1900.

61 Cup-shaped Tiffany vase, with twisted heavy gold iridescent applied decoration. Signed 'L.C.T. K 298'. Height 17 cm, c. 1899.

62 Tiffany vase, sealing-wax red with dark brown and green abstract design in the glass. Signed 'O - 2941 L.C.T.'. Height 20.3 cm, c. 1900.

63 Dark green Tiffany vase, with blue casing and purple iridescence, decorated with a silver wave-like motif. Signed 'R 1280 L.C.T.'. Height 16.5 cm, 1902.

64 Dark blue Tiffany plant pot, with iridescent gold interior, and green leaf pattern. Signed '3375 D.L.C. Tiffany - Favrile'. Height 10.5 cm, 1909.

Iridescent Glass

In his trade brochure for the Paris Exhibition, Tiffany wrote 'To achieve metallic or iridescent effects, the glass should be held over metal-oxide fumes whilst still hot; the fumes act upon the surface of the glass and leave a thin deposit which clouds its transparency and leaves behind a rainbow effect'. Later on Tiffany makes reference to the fact that this process involves a strong element of chance and that the effect varies from piece to piece. Tiffany used metallic gold lustre for tableware, drinking glasses and vases of various sorts; one of his most popular kinds of vase was made of blue-green glass with sinuous, silvery plant decoration. Technically speaking the most complicated form of decoration was the peacock-feather pattern, which was made by pulling pale feathery threads of glass over a blue ground, after which a 'peacock eye' motif was inlaid into the surface of the glass. This whole process of working a pattern into glass, took place (just as in the case of fine 'feathering) while the glass was still hot and pliable. Other simpler decorations included applied acanthus scroll decoration, decorative knobs, or a dimpled effect achieved by pinching the glass (see plate 68).

If one compares different examples of the same model (sometimes it is only possible to do this by comparing photographs), one notices subtle differences of colour and shape; for the experienced collector these variations play an important part in the evaluation of an individual piece.

Paperweight Glass

A study of the techniques used to make paperweights gives one a good idea of how a polychrome pattern becomes a harmonious entity, despite the various separate processes used in the making of it. Usually the multi-coloured patterns in the glass look completely flat as they are cased beneath a clear layer of glass. The flower effects seen in paperweights are achieved by the following process. Different coloured rods of glass are fused together in a melting process and then sliced cross-sectionally before being laid into the body of the glass. The temperature at which this operation is carried out allows for a certain movement in the glass which causes the colours to spread and make flower-like patterns (see plate 66). It was Tiffany's idea to incorporate this process, similar to the one used in Baccarat or St. Louis paperweights, into some of his vases. Paperweights were produced in great quantities

65 Golden yellow Tiffany Jack-in-the-Pulpit vase, with gold iridescence. Signed 'L.C.T. Y 3795.' Height 46 cm. 1904.

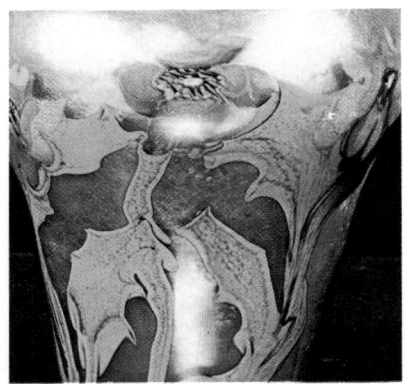

66 Detail of a Tiffany paperweight vase with *'Millefiori'* inclusions, stylized flower patterns and iridescent surface. Signed '8520 N/L. C. Tiffany Inc. Favrile'. Height 14 cm, c.1900.

67 Small amphora-shaped Tiffany vase with applied handles. Yellow glass with gold iridescence. Signed 'L.C. Tiffany - Favrile/5138E'. Height 21.8 cm, 1913.

in the nineteenth century and the same process was used whereby coloured rods were fused together to make decorative patterns and were then inlaid into semi-circular cut crystal paperweights.

Flower-Form Vases

The large flower-form vases are real works of art - they are purely decorative, and miraculous technical feats. They are often as much as 40 centimetres high, and are a sort of glass sculpture. Leafy patterns of green, white and honey colour are coaxed into the liquid substance with the utmost skill by the glass-blower. The effect of fine veining is a particular joy, and it is interesting to analyse the techniques involved in the composition of such patterns, and to observe how the many separate colours in each piece harmonise and become one. The decoration is alive and vibrant, with surprising asymetrical effects. The shapes of Tiffany glass are organic, and never have any of the stiffness and lifelessness of cut crystal. The hand of the master is seen in these refinements, and Tiffany's poetic nature and artistic training come across in every piece of glass. This is even more pronounced when Tiffany uses his techniques to achieve corrosive effects, where the surface of the glass resembles smouldering volcanic lava. In this type of glass each piece is unique. These artistically contrived effects make each piece a collector's item, which is both unique, beautiful and very valuable.

68/69 Tiffany miniature vases. *Top left*: Vase with applied knobs and peacock feather iridescence, decorated with a wavy silver band. Signed '0 4121'. Height 7 cm, *c.* 1900. 'Folded' vase with variegated iridescent surface. Signed 'L.C.T. K 578'. Height 7.5 cm, 1899. Gold lustre vase with green leaves. Signed 'H 8 L.C. Tiffany Favrile'. Height 6.5 cm, 1897. Gold lustre vase with dimpled neck. Signed '3690 H.L.C. Tiffany Favrile'. Height 7.5 cm, 1913.

'Jack-in-the-Pulpit and Goose-neck Vases'

The Jack-in-the-Pulpit Vase is the most original of Tiffany's shapes. This is a purely decorative object; a long stem rises from a circular foot which broadens out dramatically at the neck forming a kind of exaggerated decorative collar. The collar is decorated with kaleidoscopic colour effects. During the shaping of the hot glass, the exaggerated 'collar' is pulled and manipulated to look like a large orchid bloom which opens out dramatically on one side. Shimmering iridescence emphasises its exotic organic shape.

The goose-neck vase is also asymetric and is based on an eighteenth century shape used for rose-water sprinklers. A long stem rises from a bulbous base and terminates in a bill-shaped neck. The overall effect resembles the sinuous line of a goose-neck, hence the term that has been coined to describe this shape. In Bohemia Loetz copied this remarkable shape in some of his vases.

Cypriote and Lava Glass

On the surfaces of Cypriote and Lava glass an attempt was made to copy the deposits found by archaeologists on ancient glass. A crackled effect is achieved by blowing in a certain way and the surface is then dragged with coloured powdery strands. In close-up, the deposits look like miniature moonscapes. Simple shapes and outlines were chosen for these vases to make it easier to achieve crater-like depressions on the surface of the glass.

Imitators of Tiffany

Tiffany's success spurred on many other glass manufacturers to produce glass of a similar nature. Shortly after the turn of the century, an American firm by the name of 'Quezal' began to produce iridescent Tiffany-style glass with feathering and fine delicate lustre. This was produced by some former employees of Tiffany who started a small glassworks of their own in Brooklyn and named it after the South American Colibri the 'Quezal'.

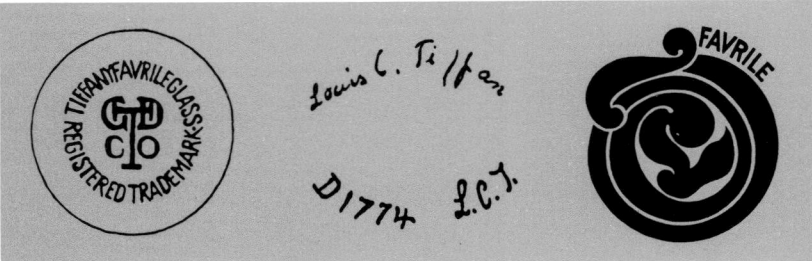

Signatures and Marks

Various marks used by Tiffany

Virtually every piece of glass made by the Tiffany studios is signed with the initials L.C.T. or signed in full Louis Comfort Tiffany. It is a well-known fact that Tiffany himself did not sign the glass. In addition to the script signature there was an inventory number which was recorded when the glass left the studio. The number had four digits, and was preceded by a capital letter. By 1905 the alphabet had been exhausted and the process was then reversed so that the letter followed the number.

The predominant colours of this thin glass were shimmering greens, golds and whites. They are signed 'Quezal' at the pontil. It is easy to confuse this with a similar type of glass made in Corning in the State of New York. Steuben too produced vases similar in style to Tiffany glass; they made lightweight flower-form vases, vases with millefiori inclusions and green and blue glass with wavy decorations. Usually this lightweight glass was gilded inside.

Art Nouveau in France

For the glass collector, French Art Nouveau glass has always been considered the most important on the international glass market. The French Art Nouveau movement was inspired not so much by architectural design as by the rich ornamentation of modern poster design, and to a lesser extent by glass design. It was in these two fields that the purest forms of Art Nouveau were to be found, and which were truly deserving of the name given to this style of design (the translation of the French term meaning of course 'The New Art Form'). The movement was immensely popular at the time, and there were many imitators of the master designers who had originated and excelled in the style. Today there is a buoyant market for Art Nouveau objects, although as with all antiques, there is a dearth of top quality merchandise. Even though prices for the most important pieces have reached astronomical heights, the demand still grows.

There were two important glass centres during the Art Nouveau period, both of them outside Paris. One of these was Nancy, now famous for the style of glass that originated there. The most important glassworks there were those of Emile Gallé, the Daum Brothers, the Muller Brothers, and Schneider Glass. Around Paris there were very few glassworks interested in the manufacture of art glass.

Rousseau/Léveillé

The glass of Eugène Rousseau (1827-1891) is considered by experts in the field to have been one of the most important forerunners of the new style that came into being at the turn of the century. His glass is thick and

70 Shown from left to right in the double page illustration on the following pages are: yellow vase with applied handles and attached feet, by Schneider, Lunéville, with coloured etched overlay decoration. Height 38 cm.
Cameo glass vase by Muller Croismaire, with carved and etched lotus-blossom pattern. Height 38 cm.
Daum Bros. bowl in mottled dark blue and yellow glass. Width 26 cm.
Egg-shell thin bowl in *pâte d'émail* by Décorchemont. Height 9 cm.
Marquetry vase by Emile Gallé with crocus pattern and *martelé* (hammered) effect at the base. Height 45 cm.
Tall-necked vase by Emile Gallé in lightly coloured glass with painted enamel design and applied decoration. Height 48 cm.

heavy, often with a crackled effect and with gold foil inclusions. By introducing metal oxides into the molten glass, Rousseau achieved clouded colour effects. This technique, discovered by him, was successfully developed further by his pupil Ernest Baptiste Léveillé. He also developed applied glass techniques and made a frosted, violet-coloured glass as well as amethyst glass. These artists preferred the more solid cylindrical or rectangular shapes to tapering elegance.

Joseph Brocard

Another glass designer who paved the way for Art Nouveau was Joseph Brocard (died 1895). He began his career in Paris as a restorer, but later turned to making glass in the Islamic or Persian style, with finely painted enamel designs. Gallé modelled his early pieces on Brocard's style. Around 1880 Brocard went from using abstract decorative shapes to more organic shapes inspired by the plant world. His glass (which is always signed), was a precursor of the Art Nouveau style.

Legras & Co.

The firm of Legras in Saint Denis produced beautiful decorative cameo glass with etched floral and landscape decoration. The pieces are usually large and decorative and signed 'Legras' in script. After the First World War they changed to a new style and produced geometric, acid-etched, Art Deco designs in thick opaque glass.

Emile Gallé - The Great Innovator

Emile Gallé changed the fundamental principles of glass manufacture and design, and evolved his own grammar and language of glass. He set off in a completely new direction where many were to follow. His name is synonymous with a highly evolved personal style, and is as important in the history of glass as the Pre-Raphaelites in the history of Victorian painting or Khnopff and Toorop in the Symbolist Movement. He was born on May 4th, 1846, in Nancy, the provincial capital of Lorraine, and grew up there during the period of the second Reich. In 1871, when he was just 25, the greater part of his native province of Lorraine was annexed to Germany, as a result of the Treaty of Versailles that followed the Franco-Prussian War. Gallé was undoubtedly one of the most engaging personalities in the art-

71 Goblet by Albert Dammouse in wrought iron mount by Nico Frères (designed by Felix Gilon). The dancing female figures are *pâte de verre*. The foot of this piece is ivory, 1910.

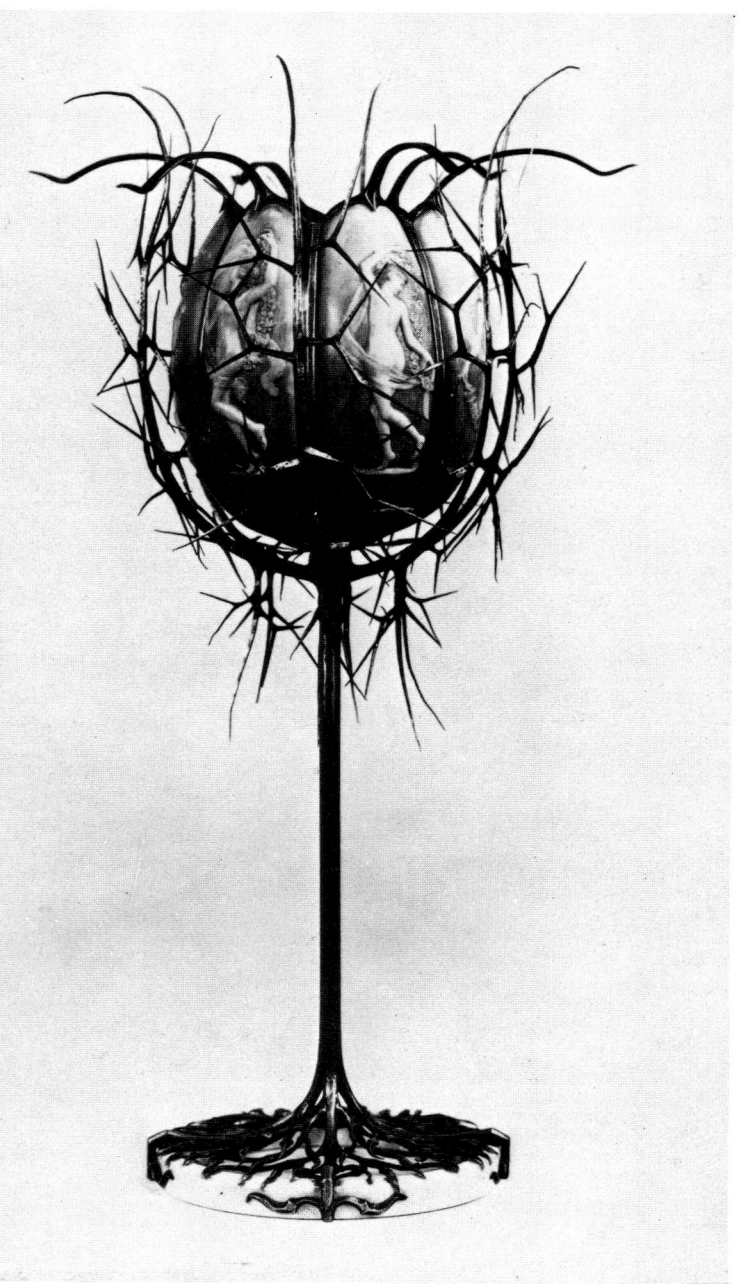

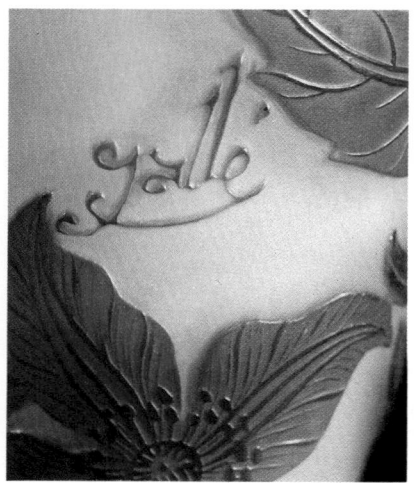

72 Signature on a commercially produced Gallé vase. The trained eye can distinguish between an industrial signature and an artist signed piece: but in either case the calligraphy of the signature forms part of the decoration, as in a Japanese painting. Carved dedications or quotations sometimes appear on unique pieces. The pieces made after Gallé's death in 1904 have a little star in front of the . signature.

world of the time. At the age of 43, at the height of his career, he turned his attention to Art Nouveau, and worked in that style for 15 years, and was among the founder members of the movement. His life was one of contrasts, changes, and even one of contradictions, when one considers his various different styles. For there is a philosophical and poetic side to Gallé's work too, which gives it depth and makes it transcend contradictions of style, so that, in a sense, contradiction becomes the very essence of his creative genius. His work is distinguished by a strength of purpose and single-mindedness that gives it a harmonious beauty. It was his aim to try and express the spirit of the age in a new language in which it is necessary to become conversant to appreciate his art. In a way his courage is

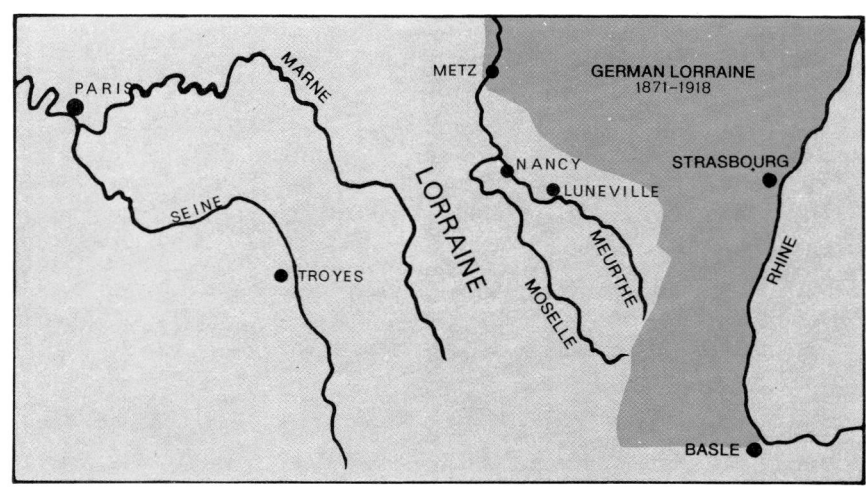

comparable to the forceful single-mindedness of Wagner's struggle against the accepted musical language of the day; in both cases their genius lay in their unswerving determination; (incidentally Gallé was a lifelong fan of Wagner). The comparison with Wagner can be taken a step further, for even today one is either a total Wagner devotee, or else one cannot bear to listen to his music at all. The same can be said of Gallé's work.

In his later years, when his health was failing (he died of Leukaemia at the age of 58 in 1904), Gallé often claimed that the powers of nature were his life-force and his inspiration, and that he wished his work to show an integrity which might influence others in his time. The arts in Paris at the time were indeed suffering from a lack of moral conviction.

The seriousness of Gallé's moral code (he earnestly claimed his idealism to be the essence of his art), made him the lampoonist's frequent target.

Gallé had beliefs, philosophies, and above all a sense of mission. He was both the inventor of a glass style, and also, thanks to his versatility and the strength of his personality, the founder of a school which came to be called the 'Ecole de Nancy', and which embodied the combined creative talents of the area.

74 Emile Gallé in his studio, painted by his friend Victor Prouvé, 1892. Prouvé's portrait paints an idealised picture both of Gallé and his work. This painting was exhibited at the Paris Exhibition in 1900.

Ecole de Nancy: A typical Art Nouveau Art Movement

With the founding of the *Ecole de Nancy*, the provincial capital Nancy experienced a blossoming of creative talent which was a typical feature of the Art Nouveau era. It is evident from the schools of design in Darmstadt, Vienna or

Glasgow that Art Nouveau was never confined to national frontiers. The beauty of a movement starting in one particular geographical location in this way, is that it starts off by developing local stylistic traditions which later evolve to become an international style as it crosses new borders.

The *Ecole de Nancy* with Emile Gallé as its figurehead is without doubt one of the most important of the many 'secessionist' movements which came into being during the Art Nouveau period.

One of the remarkable characteristics of these schools of design was the feeling of mutual admiration and solidarity shared by their members; like the members of the Nancy School, they were usually of the same generation and had consequently shared similar experiences and made similar discoveries. Other friends and members of the *'Ecole de Nancy'* included Eugène Vallin (born 1856) and Louis Majorelle (born 1859) both of whom were outstanding designers and cabinet makers, August Daum (born 1858) who like Gallé specialized in glass, and Victor Prouvé (born 1858) whose talents were many-sided and who became the figurehead after Gallé's death in 1904.

Most of Gallé's work, and that of his colleagues, drew on the scenery, animal and plant-life of Lorraine for its inspiration.

Gallé himself had a beautiful garden at this three-storey villa, where he grew all kinds of plants, and these were the source of inspiration for the plant-forms in his glass designs. Living amid such beautiful scenery, these artists used the natural wonders surrounding them in their work; the hidden beauties of nature which they were forever discovering were an endless source of inspiration to them and were worked into their designs. Many artists of the day clamped down on this and called it a form of escapism from the problems of the day. In retrospect there was indeed a sort of stubbornness in ignoring industrial progress with attitudes such as theirs. *'Ma racine est au fond des bois'*, 'My roots are in the depth of the forest', was one of the poetic principles expounded by Gallé; in so doing he proved how little he was in tune with the spirit of the Industrial Revolution. On the contrary he tended towards divine mysticism and the laws of nature, and shunned what he considered the trivialities of everyday life and human contact. What today smacks of 'hubris', was hardly intended that way when Gallé's friend Eugène Vallin carved the 'depth of the forest' motto into the oak doors of Gallé's factory.

It is an interesting fact about the *Ecole de Nancy* that its members did not work in the isolated

75 Glass furnace constructed by Gallé for the Paris World Fair in 1900. Note the decorative arrangement of broken vases, half-finished articles, and carefully arranged tools of the trade - all of which are evidence of how Gallé brought his aesthetic eye to everything he did. Above the furnace was a quotation from Hesiod, intended to reflect his own philosophy! 'Woe to man if he is evil, false, and disloyal! Come forth, ye angry demons of fire! Make vases shatter and furnaces explode. In the end man will learn justice.'

cities of France. To this extent they were combining artistic ideals with a production programme that made use of modern industrial reform. Bankers and rich patrons offered their backing to these 'industries of art', and were, in part, responsible for the successful and profitable management of the companies with which they were involved. The publisher J.B. Eugène Corbin (1867-1932) was an ardent admirer of Gallé's work, and it is in his Art Nouveau villa (preserved in its original state) that the *Ecole de Nancy* Museum is situated at the present time.

It is unthinkable that Gallé would have carved his famous *'Aube et Crépuscule'* (Dawn and Dusk) 'Butterfly Wing' bed, had he not had a specific commission from his patron Henri Hirsch. Plate 135 shows a glass lamp specially commissioned by Corbin in 1904, and executed by Gallé when he was already critically ill and confined to a wheel-chair.

Gallé spent his whole life in Nancy, and from beginning to end lived there as a perfectly ordinary middle-class citizen. But on his trips to Paris he had a taste of the eccentricities of aristocratic and artistic circles.

Gallé's parents owned several factories. His father had married into a family that owned a mirror factory and which also produced glass for household use. Gallé

atmosphere of the artist's studio. Many of them owned factories and were successful industrialists. But the products they were manu-facturing existed for aesthetic purposes alone and hardly took into account the implications of an industrial age.

Majorelle and Daum, as well as Gallé himself, ran large companies, with outlets in most of the major

managed the factory, where they also produced glass to their own designs, and the success of this venture encouraged him to take over a porcelain company that had gone bankrupt. Emile Gallé was brought up in these well-to-do surroundings, and had a strict Protestant upbringing which gave him the moral principles that influenced his working and thinking in later life.

His further education was not confined to the arts. He studied botany and art history. His studies took him to Germany and England. He later spent some time at the German glass factory of Burgen and Schverer in order to study the chemistry of glass and to become acquainted with all aspects of glass production. Later on Gallé had a secret arrangement with Burgen and Schverer whereby many of his pieces were produced by them under licence.

Apart from being a student of botany, chemistry and art history, Gallé was a young romantic, and this romanticism always remained an important factor in his work, and a determining influence in his designs. He was known in literary and artistic circles in Paris as a romantic artist skilled in the art of glass. He was one of a circle of friends that grew up around Robert de Montesquiou (1885-1921), and it was through him that Gallé made the acquaintance of the young

Marcel Proust. Eccentricity and decadence are other sides of Gallé's complex personality. The German literary critic Willy Haas sums up the whole Montesquiou-Proust milieu very perceptively: 'Montesquiou was a man who basked in his own arrogance, felt smug at the flattering mentions made of him by Proust in his letters and was both a showman and a dandy. He thought his writings were the essence of contemporary French poetry, whereas in reality his personality served more as a literary model for others. The Baron des Esseintes in Joris-Karl Huysman's *'A Rebours'* was based on him, and he served as a model for the spate of self-indulgent and eccentric dandies in literature up until Oscar Wilde's *Dorian Gray*, and even a decade later than that as the perverse main character in Proust's great social commentary, *A La Recherche du temps perdu*. Gallé's life too would have been good material for a novel; as an aesthete he moved among the dandies in Paris, and at home in Nancy he was the guiding light among glass designers; he was a Wagner fan, he was a sick man like Proust, a dreamer and a romantic but with a strong puritan streak, and a supporter of the cause of the French Jewish staff-officer Alfred Drefus. Apart from all this he was responsible for his beautiful 'Poems in Glass', and an

76 The double plate on the preceding pages shows vases, scent bottles and bowls by Emile Gallé, all c. 1900. *From left to right:* 'Butterfly vase' in intarsia glass with marquetry decoration of butterflies. Height 53 cm. Scent bottle in reddish orange glass with applied decoration in different colours. Height 32 cm. Amber coloured glass shell. Yellowish-green bowl with applied decoration. Diameter 42 cm. Small vase with applied glass shell decoration. Height 12 cm. Tall-necked vase with foil inclusions, and applied teardrop decoration; with carved floral design (the flower heads being at the base of the vase, giving them a 'drooping' impression). This sort of symbolist expressionism was often used by Gallé.

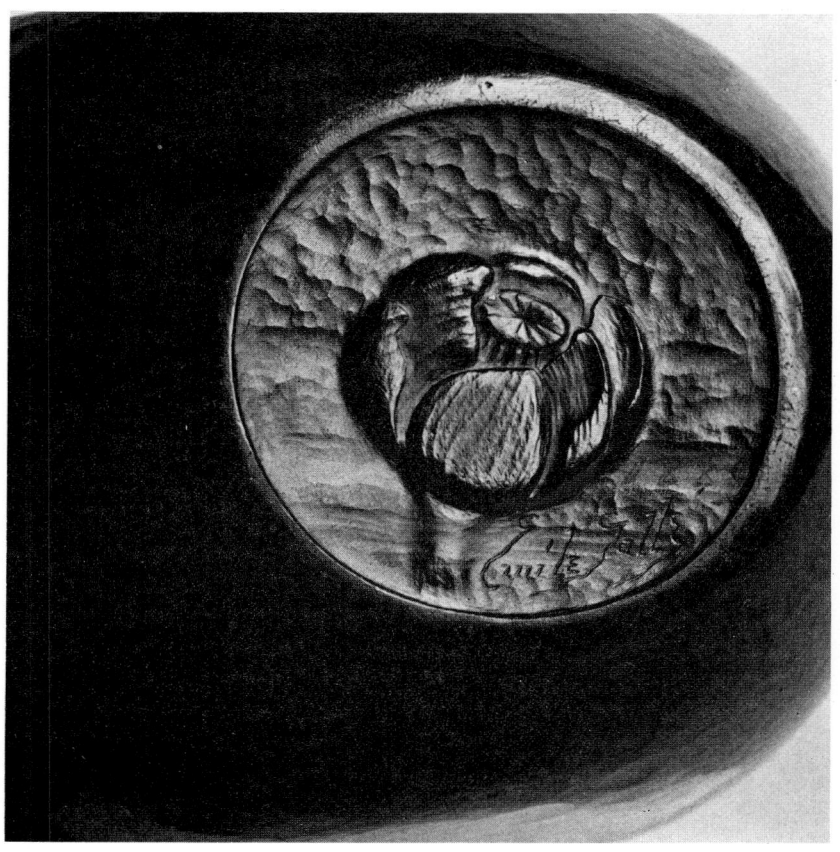

77 Detail of signature on a *'Vase de Tristesse'* ('Vase of Mourning') made of dark violet 'Hyalith' glass. 15.5 cm. As suggested by its name, this type of vase was meant to convey a mood of melancholy and sadness.

entrepreneur with a well-organized factory to his credit. But Gallé and the whole *Ecole de Nancy* would have never achieved their enormous success had it not been for their strenuous attempts to combine art and industry. The manufacture of Gallé glass in studios that were really more like 'Factories of Art' was the result of Gallé's own economic and cultural thinking, a happy marriage between artistic eccentricity and the middle class free enterprise.

Design, Production and Sales

Manufacturing a piece of Gallé glass was a matter of producing an object whose shape, colour and design combined to form a harmonious entity. His glass was, so to speak, a line from a poem translated into visual terms (he found particular inspiration in the poetry of Baudelaire), or else it was the result of direct inspiration from the natural forms of the plant world. He was fascinated too by the idea of his glass actually being

78 Scent bottle, modelled as two birds and made of several layers of cameo glass. The removable heads form the stoppers. With carved wooden base. Height 13.5 cm, Nancy 1898.

79 Gallé vase. Pale green glass with dark red overlay, and etched flower pattern. Height 49.5 cm, *c.* 1900.

80 Detail from a typical 'industrial' Gallé vase. Two colour cameo glass with etched brown landscape on a yellow ground.

81 Detail from a typical 'industrial' Gallé vase. The dragonfly is etched into the top layer of orange glass.

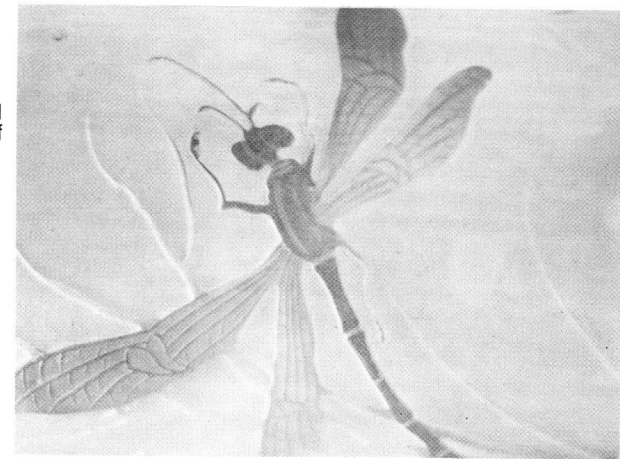

82 Detail from a Gallé marquetry vase. The fine veining of the body is cased between two layers of glass.

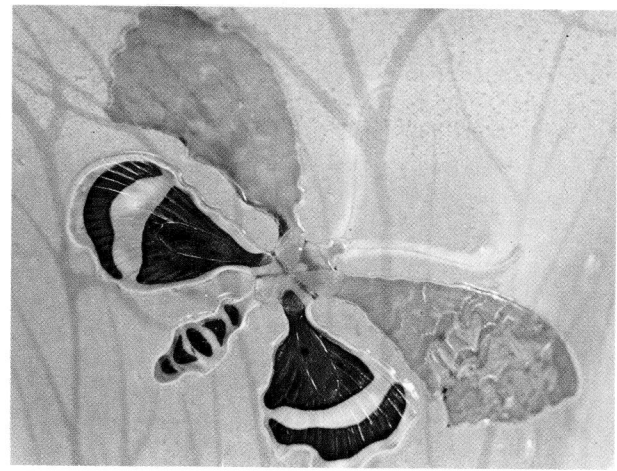

able to express thought. Technically speaking this was a matter of combining textures and colours of glass. He mixed clear glass and coloured, and the various layers of glass were combined to form organic shapes reminiscent of flowering plants or creations from the insect world.

These freely developed shapes and patterns have a strength and an impact which is partially retained even in more commercial pieces of Gallé glass and in the models turned out in large editions for the mass market.

To make sure of this he developed reliable, detailed chemical formulas, so that the most subtle colour effects could be accurately programmed, and enabled his workers to recreate his artistic intentions with accuracy.

An equally important factor with Gallé was the carving carried out on the completed body of the glass. Over the years Gallé developed techniques for doing this, and for which he took out a patent. The illustrations in plate 11 show workers in operation at the factory. Considering the detailed planning and organisation that went into the process of converting detailed works of art into commercial products, it is not surprising to find that by the turn of the century Gallé had 300 skilled employees. Most of them remained anonymous, and the glass was simply signed

'Gallé'. The only time that any of his workers had a share of the limelight was at the Paris Exhibition of 1900 where four of his men received silver medals for their excellent workmanship. These were Albert Daigueperce, Emile Munier, Julien Roiseux and Paul Oldenbach. Ten more of his workers received diplomas of merit or bronze medals on this occasion. Louis Hertoux also made a name for himself as a designer, and Auguste Herbst became renowned for his skills as a carver and acid-etcher, as did Paul Nicolas who later worked for Baccarat under his own name.

Gallé's own workmanship however overshadowed the skills of any one of his employees, and this was reflected in the price of a piece carved by the master himself. His name was heavily featured in the firm's publicity. He felt that the manufacturing process was only half the story, and that the organisation of sales was of equal importance.

Each piece was intended to carry a personal message or philosophy which would in a sense involve the buyer in Gallé's own moral and aesthetic commitment. The inscriptions on Gallé glass are often directed at the eventual owner.

He concentrated on every last detail of production, including publicity, which was always planned

83 *'L'Orchidée'* ('The Orchid'). Carved vase by Emile Gallé, with applied decoration, exhibited at the 1900 World Fair.

Munich. For the 1900 World Fair in Paris, at the height of his career, he built a glass showroom with carefully designed showcases, and a special decorative furnace to give the viewers an insight into his working world. From plate 75 we see that even here his public was confronted with moral sayings. An inscription was intended to remind the viewer of the purifying force of fire.

The photograph shows a rather too deliberately tasteful arrangement of the working tools, but is an interesting record in that it illustrates the wooden and metal moulds which Gallé used to shape his glass. A more sombre view of a subject, which had been somewhat romanticised for the purpose of the exhibition, is seen in the actual photographs of the factory (plate 11). Museums and private collectors purchased the best pieces at these exhibitions, but the Fairs also boosted sales in general. By 1885 Gallé had already opened show-rooms in Paris, and by 1897 he followed suit with one in Frankfurt, and shortly afterwards one in London.

The company's most important work was undoubtedly done during his lifetime, although even during this period there is a distinction between the pieces done by his own hand and those done by skilled employees. In general however all pieces were of an

to build him into the star who played the leading role. One must not underestimate the importance he attached to the major World Fairs, and he often spent an entire year working on an exhibit for one of these fairs. In 1884 he exhibited a group of vases entitled 'Stone-Wood-Earth-Glass' for which he received a gold medal.

He received the 'Grand Prix' at the Paris World Fair in 1889 and was also decorated with the Légion d'Honneur. In 1883 he took part in the Chicago World Fair, exhibiting glass and furniture, and in 1897 he exhibited his 'Art Nouveau' in

84/85 Gallé vase. Milky white glass overlaid with carmine red. The top layer has been etched in varying depths. The three dimensional effect comes from the varying degrees of transparency (depending on the varying thicknesses of red). The flowers are inset with lightly faceted lapis-coloured glass applications. The vase has a decorative silver band at the neck, but in general one should be wary of this type of silver decoration as it is sometimes used to conceal damage. Height 21.5 cm, Nancy c. 1900.

extremely high standard and the quality only suffered when the company went into a decline after his death in 1904. Gallé was without doubt the guiding light and source of inspiration; his glass had a particular form of idealism and magic only traces of which remain in the later commercially produced pieces. Undoubtedly the glass-blowers working for him were inspired by his commanding presence, despite the fact that he had never been a blower himself.

Gallé Glass from 1873-1931

Despite a complexity and diversity of styles, Gallé glass can be clearly divided into various periods determined by the different techniques used during each of these periods. Although these periods tend to overlap, somebody with a reasonably experienced eye will have no difficulty in dating a

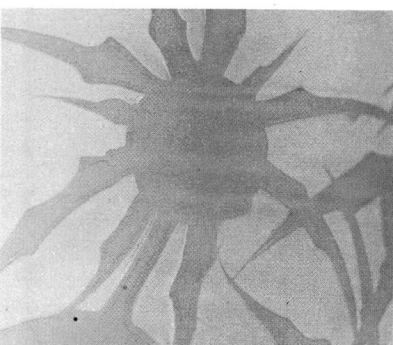

86/87 Floor vase by Gallé. Two colour cameo glass with milky white ground, and pale green etched thistle decoration. The piece is recognizable as 'industrial' Gallé, from the lack of sharpness in the outlines of the decoration; this was the result of stencilling as opposed to etching by hand. This is typical of Gallé produced between 1900 and 1931. Height 45.6 cm, Nancy 1900 - 1935.

piece of glass according to the specific techniques used.

Clear glass with painted enamel decoration. Gallé did not work in coloured glass during his earliest period; he worked in clear glass which had painted enamel decoration. The early period lasted from about 1873 to about 1875. This type of glass often comes up for sale on the art market. The pieces have either an engraved or enamelled signature, often accompanied by the Cross of Lorraine. Glass of this sort is essentially conservative in shape and based on earlier styles. It is only the decoration that hints at an attempt to find new forms of expression. There are jugs, bowls, vases and goblets, decorated with ornamental hunting scenes, thistle decoration, insects and leaf designs, and sometimes medieval figures. The more interesting and unusual forms of decoration employed by Gallé at this period were those in which he used oriental motifs. It was the influence of Brocard that led him to do so. The vase in the shape of an oriental mosque lamp, seen in plate 88, is a good example of a style still influenced by historicism. The decoration was painted on with a brush, and applied while the glass was cooling.

Verrerie parlante. *'Verrerie Parlante'*, (literally translated meaning 'Talking Glass'), was a name Gallé himself invented for a particular series of pieces where the glass was meant to have a definitely symbolistic character. Again and again during his lifetime Gallé used flowers as the symbols that would give expression to his moral philosophies. Flowers frequently appear as *'leitmotifs'*, each with its own mood. Flowers in Gallé glass act as symbols or the embodiment of an idea. The *'Verrerie Parlante'* series includes vases which incorporate lines from Victor Hugo and Charles Baudelaire. Gallé was influenced above all by *'Les Fleurs du Mal'*. Other poets too like Rimbaud, Mallarmé, Verlaine and Gautier inspired his *'Verrerie Parlante'* series.

The transitional period 1884-1889. In 1884 Gallé exhibited a series of vases intitled *'La Pierre, Le Bois, La Terre, Le Verre'*. (Stone, Wood, Earth, Glass). The subjects suggest a new treatment of glass, and the pieces themselves represent an attempt to break free

from the traditional order of things and to seek new forms of expression. It was no longer a question of decorating glass; glass as a substance was now meant to be the expression of a concept. During this transitional period before the breakthrough to Art Nouveau, Gallé was keen to explore every possible way of imitating natural substances in glass. With the help of the chemist Bernstein he experimented with imitations of jade, quartz and agate; the results were somewhat similar in texture to Bohemian Lithyalin glass. He experimented with differing degrees

88 Enamelled Gallé vase. Both in shape and in decoration this vase is reminiscent of a medieval Persian mosque lamp. It is in clear glass with a painted enamel design and is from Gallé's early period before he developed his Art Nouveau style. Height 14.5 cm, Nancy 1885.

of density in glass, which made it possible to achieve the subtlest of effects; sometimes a flower petal or an insect's wing was modelled out of semi-translucent glass and applied on to an opaque coloured base, or the process was reversed and a semi-translucent base was decorated with applied figural shapes in opaque colours. These pieces combine a variety of different sorts of glass and are the most original and also the most valuable. In this technique Gallé treats his material as if it were watercolour paint. During this time Gallé was like a Symbolist Painter exploring every possible style and every new form of expression that could result from varying intensities of colour and light. At this period the glass was signed in relief, with a vertical signature often with exaggerated curlicues.

Glass marquetry. The technique of glass marquetry is far more risky than the production of ordinary cameo glass. The process is similar to wood marquetry, where different coloured pieces of wood veneer are bonded together and inlaid into a wooden surface to make a design. Gallé had already had experience of this technique in wood. But it was a long while before he managed to make use of a similar technique in glass. On April 26th 1898 he took out a patent in Paris for 'Glass or Crystal Marquetry'. This technique involves a process whereby different coloured glass pieces are laid onto a glass surface; it is a sort of glass on glass inlay. The difficulty lies in the fact that the different colours of glass have to melt into one another, and during this procedure, particularly during the cooling process, there are varying degrees of tension due to the differing densities of the separate colours, which often leads to the glass shattering or developing internal cracks.

When a piece of glass made in this way developed a crack, Gallé did not bother to finish the piece and yet he did not allow it to be thrown away, but had it inscribed lovingly *'Etude Gallé'*, (a Gallé study piece). Aesthetically speaking, these pieces have a certain charm in that they reveal the basic structure of the art form. Such pieces are extremely rare and much sought after by collectors.

The study pieces. The study pieces are the most experimental of Gallé's work; for an example see plates 89 and 90. Collectors attach more and more importance to these pieces for their unfinished state has a refreshing degree of improvisation not present in the finished commercial pieces. It is because of their experimental nature that they tend to be unfinished; often there is no

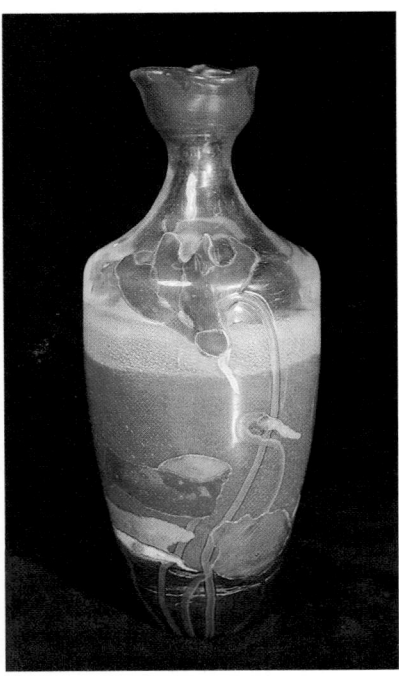

89/90 Gallé vase using the *marqueterie de verre* technique. This vase was never finished as it developed an internal crack due to stress while cooling. Hence the signature *'Gallé Etude'* (Gallé study) on the base. Height 17.5 cm, Nancy c. 1900.

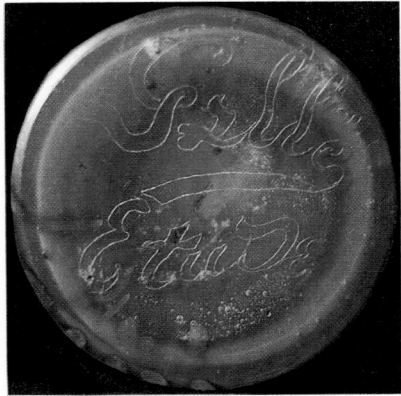

carving, and they are therefore preserved in the same state as they were when they adorned the studio shelves. They are always signed with the word *'Etude'* followed by a Gallé script signature.

Standard Gallé cameo glass. It was only possible for Art Nouveau cameo glass to be produced commercially when the technique of acid-etching was introduced; in the beginning Gallé shied away from this technique.

However towards the end of the century he agreed that a patent be taken out in his name for a process whereby it was possible to obtain a satin finish to glass; this he called *'Patine du Verre'* (glass patina). In chemical terms it is the addition of ash to the glass substance, which gives it a smooth surface texture. Acid-etching was used on this matt finish. This process was usually used on glass consisting of two layers, and is what is commonly called a piece of 'standard' Gallé glass. The pieces shown in plates 91 and 92 are good examples of this type of Art Nouveau glass.

By this method a consistently high standard was maintained, but without the added appeal of uniqueness or creative spontaneity. This kind of glass has an acid-etched signature (see plate 28) which starts at the bottom and goes diagonally upwards.

Even these pieces fetch high

prices, although they are hardly connected at all with Gallé's personal skills as a craftsman. Plates 91 and 92 are good examples of standard Gallé glass. In evaluating this kind of glass, the following criteria should be taken into consideration.

1. The botanical accuracy of the decoration.
2. Integration and harmony of decoration and shape.
3. Signature.
4 Whether the piece is two or three layer cameo glass, and how well each layer is carved.

To begin the work of decoration on a three layer piece of glass, the pattern of the top layer is painted on in an acid resistant varnish. The areas covered in this varnish will then remain intact when the piece is dipped in an acid bath and the acid eats into the parts not covered by the varnish. As the acid takes effect, the lower layer of blue glass is revealed. The process is then repeated on this layer, and the lacquer once again applied to whichever parts the acid is not meant to touch. Once again the vase is dipped in acid. After this second bath, the yellowish bottom

91/92 Gallé vase. Two colour cameo glass with clematis design. A good example of commercially produced Gallé glass intended for the mass-market. This type of vase is known as Standard Gallé. Height 46 cm, Nancy c. 1900.

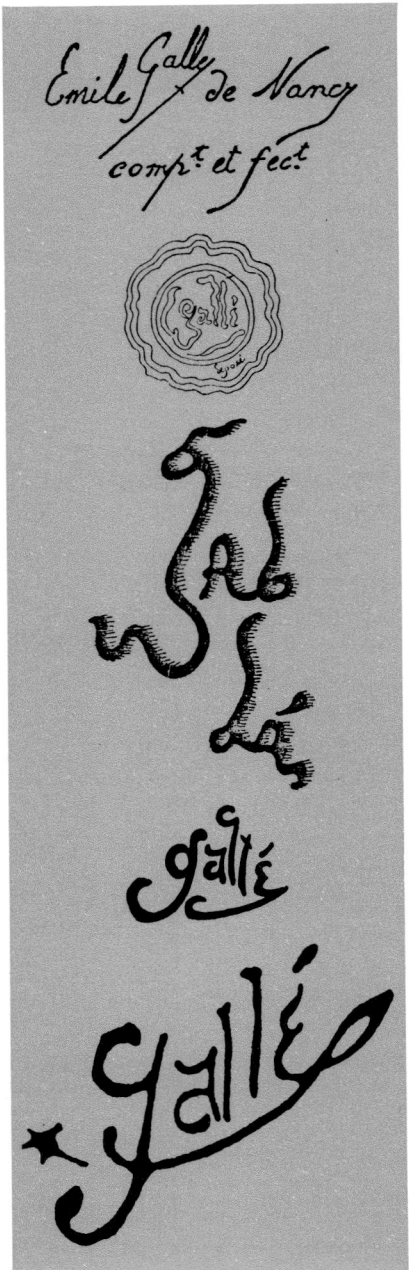

layer of glass begins to show through. The various layers are clearly visible in the end product. In floral decoration the veining of the petals is etched on the top layer of lilac coloured glass; the blue layer underneath acts like a negative, throwing the top layer of lilac into relief so that the veins stand out. With the leaves the process is reversed. The leaves are carved out of the blue layer (positive) and stand out in relief against the yellow veining (negative) of the bottom layer of glass. The stems too are composed of two layers of glass, with the paler blue of the lower layer acting as a shadow which highlights the top layer and lends added depth.

'Gallé industriel' cameo glass
'Gallé Industriel' is the collective term used to describe glass made at the factory after Gallé's death (in other words glass made between the years 1904 and 1931). The industrial pieces have two or at most three layers of glass in all. A stencil is used in these pieces to apply surface decoration before the acid bath. Only in very rare

Gallé signatures. *From top to bottom*: Early signature: signature dating from 1885-1895 of a *'piece unique'*; carved signature of an important piece c. 1900: signature etched in relief c. 1900: etched signature after 1904. The small start in front of the signature implies that the glass was manufactured after Gallé's death in 1904.

instances is any of the decoration on these pieces done by hand. The 'industrial' technique was often used for lamps as well as for vases.

Daum Nancy

The firm of Daum was founded in Nancy in 1875 and was involved in the production of decorative glassware. It made drinking glasses and reproductions of antique glass. Only in 1887, when Daum's two sons Jean-Louis-Auguste and Jean-Antonin took over the company, was part of their production geared to the manufacture of art glass. This was almost certainly as a direct result of the success of Emile Gallé.

Nowadays one usually talks of Gallé and Daum in the same breath. Both of them play an equally important role in the historic developments in glass manufacture for which the province of Lorraine was responsible during the Art Nouveau period. Although both firms shared many character-istics, the glass of each is easily distinguishable. A trained eye does not need the help of a signature to distinguish differences of technique, shape and decoration. There is no doubt that Gallé was the greater innovator and the more inspired artist, and that the most important *'pièces uniques'* were executed by him. But the larger editions of commercial glass produced by both

companies were of an equally high standard.

In 1890 the Daum glass studios in Nancy began producing vases with floral and figural decoration; they also produced beautiful landscape vases in etched cameo glass with additional enamelled decoration. Stylistically speaking their designs were typical of the *Ecole de Nancy* of which the Daum Brothers were also founder members.

There is a very distinctive type of Daum glass which makes abundant use of colour in the body of the glass: the polychrome effect was achieved by introducing coloured powdered glass or other colour additives during the smelting process. The colour structure can clearly be seen on the rough edge of a broken piece of Daum glass, when a piece of broken glass is held to the light.

This is a different technique from that used in conventional cameo glass where layers of glass are laid on top of one another; in this process different colours are mixed into the basic substance giving the body of the glass a mottled effect. Just as with cameo glass, it is possible to treat this sort of surface with acid-etching or carving. Daum also manufactured a kind of glass where this mottled glass was cased between two other layers; this came to be known as *'Verre de Jade',* (jade glass). the mottled Daum surface made a very

successful background for land-scapes and floral decoration. When exposed to a strong light the colours enclosed in the glass come to life. With this technique it is possible to achieve deeply concen-trated colour, or cloudy streaks, or most effective of all subtle shading from dark violet to pale yellow, from red to green; this has come to be thought of as one of the most attractive features of Daum glass. These colour effects were much exploited when it came to the manufacture of glass lamps, and it was because of the particular characteristics of this glass that

93 Detail of a Daum Nancy bowl, showing clearly the raised decoration done by etching. The glass substance is mixed with coloured powder to achieve a polychrome effect.

94 Daum coloured glass bowl with etched decoration. Diameter 25 cm.

95 Daum Nancy two layer cameo glass vase in yellow and brown with etched landscape design. Height 28 cm.

96 Typical signature for an 'industrial' Daum piece. The enlarged details show the poor quality and blurred outline of the etching.

97 Vases by Daum Nancy. *From left to right*: tall-necked vase with applied handles and foot in mottled glass. Height 43 cm. Typical long-necked vase in reddish yellow glass with colour powder inclusions. Height 60 cm. Slender trumpet-shaped vase with etched and carved decoration of butterflies and bats on a shaded ground. Height 47 cm, Nancy 1898.

98 View of the Daum factory in Nancy.

Daum decided to put such emphasis on the production of light fittings. Hundreds and thousands of lampshades in mottled glass were sold by Daum well into the 1920s.

This jade glass effect is also known in France as *'Pâte de Verre'*, (glass paste), though strictly speaking this is a misnomer. None the less it is a term that is in common usage (or rather misusage) in France. There is however one thing that 'jade glass' and the real *'pâte de verre'* have in common, which is that powdered glass is used for colouring in both cases; (what is meant by powdered glass is actual crushed coloured glass or 'metal oxide').

Daum liked to mix techniques in a single piece. There are for instance pieces where the body of the glass is the mottled substance described above, over which there is applied coloured glass in places. Daum did not cover the whole surface of the glass with another layer, but preferred to confine it to the areas where there was going to be relief decoration. These areas where there was a double thickness of glass were either wheel-cut or acid-etched. To make the decoration stand out, and create a three dimensional effect, parts of the pattern were painted with enamel colours. The finished product had a polychrome effect which for today's tastes might be somewhat gaudy. Daum liked to use dark murky colours, like dark green, dark orange, violet and dirty red.

But the company did not restrict itself to dark shades, and was equally successful with a cooler palette. Colour was classified by Daum according to the seasons. There were vases decorated with wintery snow scenes of forests and villages; then there were autumnal scenes with dark trees covered in autumn fruits; there were summer landscapes with bunches of flowers and gardens in full bloom, and spring-like patterns with crocus or snowdrop decoration. These landscape pieces are like paintings; in fact some of them are exact replicas óf paintings, many copied from the Dutch Masters. There are of course different categories of Daum glass, each of which is evaluated for its particular merits. There is a great difference between a piece of hand-carved cameo glass and a piece of mould-blown glass with stencilled decoration. Like Gallé, Daum produced glass ranging from unqiue artist designed pieces to mass produced editions.

Vases with wrought iron mounts.
One often sees Daum glass with wrought iron mounts. The glass-blower blows the glass into a preliminary shape which is then pressed whilst still hot and pliable into a wrought iron mount. The blowing then continues so that the glass balloons out of the various apertures of the mount and cannot be removed from its mounting once it has cooled. The firm of Louis Majorelle was chiefly responsible for these metal mounts; decorative wrought iron was their most important product after furniture which was their chief concern. Daum usually used coloured glass for these pieces; the various reds, blues, greens and shades of gold looked particularly vivid against a strong light. There are often gold metal foil inclusions in the glass used in these pieces, which gives the glass a shimmering metallic effect; the metal foil is introduced at the molten mass stage. These 'combination' pieces bear two signatures, one for each of the designers, Daum and Majorelle (see page 92).

Overlapping techniques.
'Verre intercalaire' requires perhaps the most complicated of Daum techniques; the most literal translation of 'intercalaire' is overlapping; in this context it refers to the overlapping of different techniques in a single piece of glass. Very few pieces were made in this way as it was such a risky procedure. There are various stages in this technique of glass-making. To begin with a lump of cameo glass is prepared, made up of several layers of glass, (any shape will do). Once it has cooled, this mass can be worked like any other piece of cameo glass; one can cut it with the wheel or

99 Daum vase with dark violet
overlay, carved and applied teardrop decoration. Height 29 cm,
1895-1900.

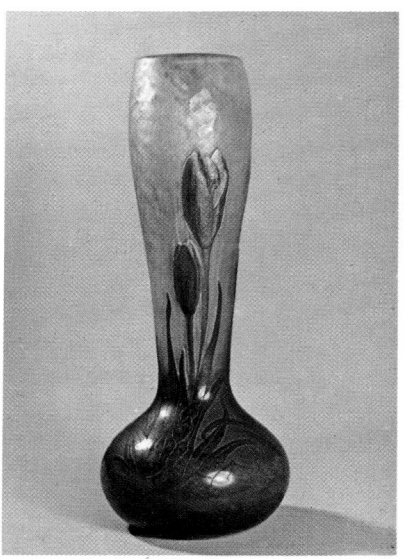

100 Daum vase. Carved crocus
decoration on a *martelé* (hammered)
blue ground. Height 25.4 cm,
c. 1900.

embellish it with enamel paint. The
next step is to re-heat this
decorated lump, and sometimes
even to add a clear layer of glass at
this stage. It is now shaped to form
the required vase, bottle or bowl.
As with Tiffany paperweight vases
the decoration is then sunk into the
glass. The difference between this
and Tiffany paperweight vases is
that Tiffany only worked to very
specific formulas, working only on
the hot glass, whereas Daum (and
the company was famous for this
sort of hybrid procedure) combined
techniques at every stage, no
matter whether the glass was hot
or cold.

At the Daum factory every possible
kind of technique was used, and
whatever the technique every piece
of Daum glass was signed. The
different signatures of Daum glass
denote different dates of production.
From 1890-1896 the glass was
usually signed with an enamel
painted signature; around 1900 the
signature was etched on to the
surface. Outstanding pieces had a
deep carved signature coupled
with the town of origin 'Nancy' and
the cross of Lorraine. As production
grew and became more commercial,
the signature changed once more.
'Daum' was written above 'Nancy',
the vertical line of the D

101 Miniature Daum vases in different colours with painted enamel decoration. Heights 2.5 - 5 cm.

extending far below the letter, with two horizontal lines crossing it near the base to form the Cross of Lorraine; the N of Nancy used this same long vertical continuation of the D as its vertical beginning, and the M of Daum swept downwards in a bar to join with the base of the vertical line of the D.

Miniature vases. It is worth saying a word or two about the miniatures, which are only a few centimetres high, and are tiny versions of the bigger vases. These small pieces are decorated with winter landscapes, coastal scenes and other miniature decoration. Even these miniatures are signed 'Daum - Nancy'. Gallé and Loetz also made miniatures at the turn of the century. Although miniatures were made in fair quantity, it is difficult to form a collection of them as they tend to be difficult to find.

Pâte-de-Verre

The literal translation of this term is 'glass-paste', which goes some way towards describing the technique used in making glass of this sort. There is no blowing of hot glass. The glass is kneaded or moulded into shape rather like clay, and then baked in an oven until it attains the consistency of glass. This pliable glass substance

is composed of ground glass bound by some sort of adhesive; the glass can be coloured to whatever shade is desired. It is particularly suitable, in the same way as porcelain, for making vases, decorative sculptural pieces, relief panels and jewellery. *Pâte de Verre* is a particularly attractive material to work in because of the endless subtle colour variations that are possible. There is never any element of hurry with this material since the glass does not need to be worked whilst hot. If a colour does not turn out to be satisfactory, it can be modified and then baked again.

The technique of *'Pâte de Verre'* was already known in ancient times as can be seen from some of the earliest pieces of Egyptian glass. Like so many crafts, it became a forgotten art, and was only re-introduced during the Art Nouveau period. Potters and sculptors found it a fascinating medium to work in.

But before the technique became general practice once more, it had to be virtually re-discovered. We have the Frenchman César Isidore Henri Cros (1840-1907) to thank

Daum Frères, Nancy signatures. *From top to bottom*: Signature from 1890-1896 applied in gold enamelling: signature *c.* 1900, etched into the surface (with cross of Lorraine): alternative signature *c.* 1900, etched into the surface (also with cross of Lorraine): signature after 1910 etched in relief. Combined Daum and Majorelle signatures.

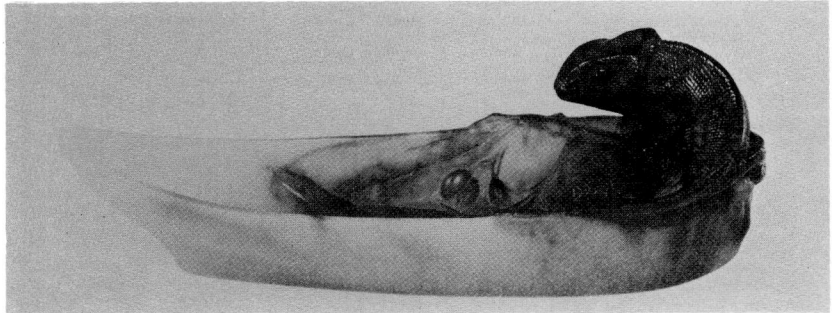

102 *Pâte de verre* dish by Almeric Walter, with life-like modelled chameleon. Signed 'Walter & Bergé. Length 25.5 cm.

for this. He came from a very distinguished family, was a classical scholar and could therefore read Pliny in the original Latin. Pliny described this 'lost art' in great detail. Cros did experiments in his own kitchen following Pliny's instructions and made a mixture of ground crystal and metal oxide, which he then baked. It required many experimental attempts before the substance reached the required consistency. It was not until, (at the recommendation of the Paris Academy), a small studio at the Sèvres porcelain factory was placed at his disposal, with a special oven that would guarantee the right temperature both for heating and cooling the substance, that he met with any success.

Henri Cros made mainly statues and plaques with relief decoration after classical models, he exhibited these and was finally rewarded for his efforts in 1895 with the Legion d'Honneur. Examples of his work are extremely rare.

Albert Dammouse (1848-1926) was equally important. He too designed ceramics for Sèvres and Haviland, before concentrating on *pâte de verre* in the 1890s. Both his taste and the style of his work (see plate 71) are unmistakably those of an artist used to working in ceramics. His graceful dancing figures are sculpted in fine relief, in the manner of the famous *pâte sur pâte* Sèvres style.

To begin with his work was inspired by classical statuary, but in due course his *pâte de verre* figures took on a remarkable realism. The little sea-creatures, insects and plants he modelled in *pâte de verre* were completely realistic, despite the bizarre texture of the material of which they were made. A very early example of this naturalistic style is seen in the vase by the Belgian artist Georges

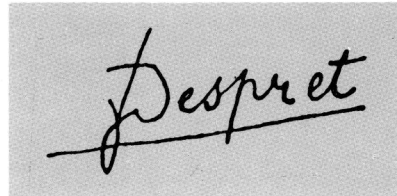

103/4 *Pâte de verre* vase by Décorchemont, blue body with dark blue and green ground glass inclusions. Impressed mark 'DECORCHEMONT'. Height 8.8 cm.

105/106 *Pâte de verre* bowl by Argy-Rousseau, with band of geometric decoration in shades of yellow red and brown. Mounted on a silver base. Height 13 cm, Paris 1925-30.

107/8 Yellow *pâte de verre* vase by Gabriel Argy-Rousseau, with stylized floral decoration. Height 25 cm, 1919-1925.

109 Important *pâte de verre* vase by Georges Despret. With low relief decoration of seaweed and starfish and two handles modelled as stylized sea-horses. Signed 'Despret, No 1163'. Height 21 cm, dating from 1905, his most important period.

Signature of Despret

Despret (1862-1952), illustrated in plate 109. The handles are in the shape of little sea-horses and both the star-fish and the sea-weed depicted on the body of the vase are realistic in shape and in scale; only the colouring bears no relation to reality.

Despret, who owned glassworks, started very early on in his career experimenting with *pâte de verre*. He had glass powder ground from broken bits of glass, which he re-formed as a workable substance; it was then modelled and fired. His experiments encouraged many of the sculptors and artists working for him to try their own experiments. Pieces signed Despret are fairly rare, as it was not his intention that the pieces be offered for sale.

One of the most important artists in *pâte de verre* was François Emile Décorchement (1880-1971). His pieces are real collectors' items and they are beautiful but expensive. They are all signed and numbered, and were made in strictly limited editions. He mixed his own substances and improved the formula for the basic material so that it became much more durable. The secret of his success lay partly in finding the correct proportions for the mixture, but also in discovering the correct temperature for firing.

Décorchement first fired his pieces in a medium heat; they were then examined carefully for any flaws, and then re-fired at a temperature of 1200° so that they became a homogeneous mass in the melting process. It was necessary to fire them in the oven for 20 hours at this high temperature. The cooling process took several days; it had to be done gradually, for otherwise the glass would run the risk of cracking or shattering. Before the massive geometric shapes of his Art Deco period, Décorchement had developed a technique for making lightweight pieces which he decorated with finely modelled plant-forms in relief.

The work from the studio of

Mark of Décorchement

Mark of G. Argy Rousseau

Almaric Walter of Nancy (1859-1942) was truly remarkable for its realism. He began his career by working at the Daum factory from 1906 to 1914, and after the war started up a little workshop of his own in Nancy. As a member of the *Ecole de Nancy* he maintained close contact with his former employer, and the chief designer at Daum (Henri Bergé) also designed models for Walter. The earliest pieces are for that reason signed Daum, but later on they were signed both 'A. Walter' and 'H. Bergé'.

These pieces are very popular with collectors as they were produced in considerable quantity, and are still readily available. These are charming naturalistic models, in ravishing colours, of chameleons, crabs, insects, birds and flowers. Walter also modelled small-scale statuettes. One of the more famous of these depicts Venus de Milo, and there is also the well-known dancing figure of Loie Fuller (the American veil dancer) after the original by the distinguished sculptor Victor Prouvé.

Pieces by Argy Rousseau tend on the whole to be expensive, falling between the works of Walter and Décorchement with regard to quality and price. They were made in a small factory started in 1921 by Gabriel Rousseau (1885-1953) in Paris. He too came from the world of porcelain manufacture.

Rousseau's work is somewhat more stylized than that of Walter although both of them used more or less the same subject-matter: Rousseau decorated his work with stylized flowers, butterflies and fruit, as well as with classical figures. From a purely artistic point of view the dancing figures are probably his best work.

With the rising demand for *pâte de verre*, prices have gone up. Even the more common mass-produced models have been fetching respectable prices, and one-off pieces fetch ten times more.

Mark of A. Walter

Mark of Dammouse

Art Glass in the 1920's and 1930's

The decorative arts of the years between the wars saw as many changes in shape and style as the era of Art Nouveau that preceded it. Art Nouveau expressed itself in poetic imagery and organic shapes; by contrast the colour combinations of the Art Deco period became more and more daring, and no shape was considered too bizarre. It was the age of glamour, the Jazz age, the Charleston era. 'Anything Goes' was one of the catch-phrases of the period, and this was certainly the case when it came to artistic decoration, whether on vases, cocktail glasses, glass lamps, scent bottles, or ornamental figures. Madness was in the air, and nothing was considered too extraordinary. No surface escaped the decorator's hand and everything from cigarette cases to fabric, and from aeroplane interiors to costume jewellery was a riot of Ziggurats, geometric patterns, stylized flowers and flapper figures. 'Tango' was a shade of burnt orange that appeared everywhere during the 1920s, and this gave way to Elsa Schiaparelli's 'Shocking Pink' in the 1930s.

It was a period when decorators could give free rein to their imagination, and many of the inspired decorative objects of the Art Deco period have found ready buyers on today's art market. One of the first books to appear on the subject was *The Decorative Twenties* by the English author, painter and set designer Martin Battersby, published in 1969; it recalled the almost purely decorative 'high camp' style of furniture, carpets, wall-coverings, fashion accessories and glass of the period. It was at the end of the 1960s that the term Art Deco began to be the accepted phrase for describing this period in the decorative arts.

Art Deco

Art Deco was not a term used to describe any particular style during the 1920s, but in recent years it has become a common international catch-phrase used to refer to the

110 The double-page illustration on the preceding page shows Lalique car mascots. *From left to right*: *'Grande Libellule'* ('Large Dragonfly'). Signed 'R. Lalique, No. 385'; *'Victoire'* ('Spirit of the Wind'), No. 1147, c. 1930; *'Tête de Aigle'* ('Eagle's Head'), No. 1138.

111 Lalique vases produced during the 1920s. All decorated in relief. Height 21-25 cm.

period of design between the wars. The name was introduced at various major exhibitions, notably the Minneapolis Exhibition of 1966 entitled 'The World of Art Deco'. Art Deco is a shortened version of *L'Exposition Internationale des Arts Décoratifs et Industriels Modernes'*, an extravagant exhibition which set a fashion for stylization and pure decoration, and did its best to eclipse other more serious avant-garde movements such as the German *Bauhaus*, or the Dutch *De Stijl* movement. Movements such as these two were against decoration for its own sake; they stripped their surfaces down to the bare bones, rid them of ornament, and concentrated on functionalism - they had no desire to be connected in any way with the 'Art Deco' trend. Today the term Art Deco is used loosely to describe the modish decorative style of the day, including a good many practical household objects, fixtures and fittings which had become revolutionized and taken on a new look as they now entered the decorator's domain for the first time in history.

Le Style 25

'Le Style 25' was the term used in France to describe the interior decor (furniture, lamps, ceramics and glass) of the time. Once again this refers to the all-important 1925 Paris *'Exposition Internationale des Arts Décoratifs et Industriels Modernes'*.

As with Art Nouveau, the glass of the Art Deco period, ranges from ordinary unsigned pieces, typical of the period, to pieces that can be called real works of art. The difference is, of course, reflected in price-structures. An ordinary piece of Art Deco glass goes for very little, whereas glass by famous designers, particularly unique pieces, can fetch astronomical sums. Between the two extremes however, there is a wide range of interesting and well-designed glass from this period. This falls into various categories:

1. Artist designed glass - above all the solid, unique glass forms designed and hand-blown by Maurice Marinot.
2. *Pâte de verre*. The work of Décorchement stands out for its excellence, followed by the larger commercial editions by Walter and Argy Rousseau (which fetch correspondingly lower prices).
3. Moulded Glass. Much of the glass produced at this time, which appears for sale at auction today, was moulded. This was simply commercially produced glass, but as in the case of René Lalique, was often designed by a top-ranking artist. Imitations of Lalique's style are rated less highly.
4. Mass produced glass. The mass-produced glassware of the day has its own charm - much of it had painted enamel decoration, and was acid-etched. Most of it was unsigned, like for instance the attractive coloured glass that was

made at the time in Bohemia; there they made geometrically shaped cut-glass vases in attractive shades of green, blue and dark violet. Bohemian glass ranges from art glass to the cheapest (but very often decorative) glassware. Art glass from Bohemia includes some that was designed by *Wiener Werkstatte* artist Josef Hoffman and Dagobert Peche, although these cannot be put in the same class as the hand-blown pieces made from start to finish by Marinot himself. Bohemian glass of the 1920s has not been nearly as well researched or documented as French art glass of the period. English glass does not play an important role in the glass of the period, although England produced some of the most original and well-designed household glass of that time. Some very interesting glass was produced, as has already been mentioned, by the Dutch Leerdam factory. German Art Deco glass includes W.M.F. glass with their 'Myra' and 'Ikora' series.

Maurice Marinot

'I believe that a beautiful piece of glass should be as far as possible the embodiment of the breath that was used to create it, and that its shape denotes a moment in time, frozen for eternity once the glass has cooled.' These words were written by Maurice Marinot (1882-

1960) who is recognized as the greatest artist in glass of the 1920s. It is not easy to understand the aesthetics of his style, for it is a personal idiom far from the norm. There is no relief decoration, and there are none of the conventionally accepted shapes. His glass is like a solid slab of nature; most pieces are enormously heavy and their mis-shapen forms might at first sight be associated with the work of first-year art students, especially when compared with the precise machine finish of commercial glass.

At first glance there seems to be no trace of craftsmanship; the lump of glass looks as if it is formed of molten lava, full of strange imperfections and secrets. 'The

112 Glass by Maurice Marinot. *From left to right:* Scent bottle in red and clear glass with miniature stopper. Face-form vase in clear glass with air bubbles. Scent bottle in heavy 'bubbled' glass, with miniature stopper. Heights 8-16 cm, *c.* 1925-1935.

real glass maker must blow the transparent mass at the furnace. He must use his lips, and the instruments that have been invented for his use. He has to work in conditions of extreme heat and dense smoke, his eyes streaming with tears and his hands burning with the intense heat.' Marinot's words struck home and impressed his contemporaries. He had given up a career as a painter, in order to devote himself to intensive research into the artistic and expressive qualities of glass. His first experiments resulted in brightly painted enamel decoration in the classical manner, and it was some time before he evolved his own style of expression. He learnt to treat glass as a sculptor treats stone; for him the glass mass was the most important factor; he thought of it as solid matter into which air bubbles could be systematically introduced for structural effects. In all Marinot made over 2500 pieces, all of which almost immediately found their way into museums and private collections. His glass was always rated very highly, and the top interior designers of the day included it in their showrooms whenever possible.

Glass of a similar nature was made by Henri Navarre (1885-1971), André Thuret (1898-1965) and Georges Du Moulin (born 1882). They all made heavy pieces, with structural effects created by the inclusion of controlled air bubbles. The Daum factory also produced some similar pieces which were heavy and monumental free-blown forms.

René Lalique

The output of René Lalique (1860-1945) was enormous and his glass makes the ideal collector's item. In contrast to Marinot, who produced a total of approximately 2500

pieces of glass during his lifetime, the firm of Lalique was famous for its high quality mass-produced art glass.

In the years between the wars alone, approximately 1500 different models of vases, figures and lamps

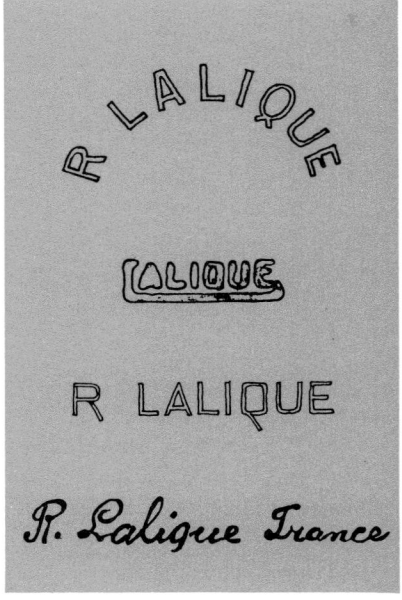

Marks of Lalique

were in production. By the 1930s, Lalique must certainly have produced more than 10 million separate pieces of glass (discounting the scent bottles the company manufactured for the perfume industry) - but this in no way jeopardised or cheapened the outstanding quality of each individual piece. For Lalique was much more than just a fashion-conscious designer.

At the turn of the century he worked as a jeweller, making specially designed pieces for a small and very distinguished clientele, and achieved world renown. Many of the pieces were commissioned by the oil millionnaire

his later work in the glass industry. He continued to retain his artistic ideals, but his attitude towards business changed fundamentally. During his Art Nouveau period Lalique had become world famous as an exclusive jeweller, during the

113 **René Lalique** (1860-1945)

Calouste Gulbenkian (1885-1957), who gave them to Sarah Bernhardt (1844-1923) to wear. Lalique's work went beyond the accepted barriers of jewellery design; they were works of art in their own right, and they were to have an important influence on the Art Nouveau movement as a whole both in concept and design.

The earlier designs of his Art Nouveau period inspired much of

1920s, however, he became renowed as one of the leading French industrialists. He catered for a keen mass-market making his own outstanding artistic designs universally available to the public. René Lalique was born in 1860 in Ay (in the province of Marne). A Viennese critic, writing of the sensational success of the jewellery exhibited by Lalique at the 1900 Paris World Fair, summed up his career as follows:

'René Lalique was no child prodigy; as a reluctant student of the fashion and design departments of the Paris School of Art (which he abandoned in 1878 at the age of 18), he was considered to have shown reasonable talent, and no more. He left Paris and went to England, where he effortlessly ran away with several important prizes. Two years later he returned to Paris where he worked for various big jewellers, doing ordinary commercial designs. Lalique owes a part of his particular talent to the detailed and painstaking studies he made of the plant and insect worlds; his knowledge in that area is always apparent from the fine detail of his decoration and design.'

The same Viennese critic remarked perceptively:

'Lalique made a detailed study of nature, as perhaps no artist before him. He made thousands of sketches, and built small scale models, which he coloured painstakingly; he studied every structural detail, noted the million subtle individual patterns of veining, colouring, and shape, and tried to discover the very breath of life that nature imparts to even its minutest creation. In this way he made a complete study of nature and became an expert on all forms of plant life from the tallest tree to the tiniest clump of moss.'

This quotation gives a clear idea of the detailed and painstaking art of Lalique, to which he devoted his whole life. Thousands of his drawings remain as documentary evidence of his detailed and studiously researched design work. A commission from Coty, the French perfume manufacturer could well have been a decisive factor in Lalique's change of direction from jewellery over to glass. He commissioned Lalique to design scent flasks for him. As early as 1906, Coty had written 'give a woman the best perfume you can mix, put it in the perfect container (it must be simple but immensely attractive), give it a reasonable price-tag, and you will see a business developing on a scale never yet known to man.' This might have acted as a catalyst for Lalique, for he saw a way in which his studio, his artistry and the hard won experience he had gained in ten years of working as a jeweller, might be used to reach a wider clientele. He began to court the market that he had studiously avoided at the turn of the century. In 1908/9 he founded his first glass-factory, called *Verrerie de Combs-La-Ville*'. But his mass-produced glass only achieved world renown around 1918-1922 when his new factory at Wingen-sur-Mode called *Verreries d'Alsace René Lalique & Cie* went into full production. His glass was one of the major sensations at the famous

114/115 *'Tourbillon'* (Whirlwind), vase by René Lalique. In turquoise glass impressed signature 'R. Lalique, France, No. 973'. Height 20.8 cm, *c.* 1925. There are various versions of this vase; one of them is in clear glass with black enamelling on raised polished surfaces. It was also made in amber glass. This model was exhibited at the 1925 Paris *'Exposition Internationale des Arts Décoratifs et Modernes'* in the category of 'artist designed industrial glass'. It is basically a moulded piece (with a mould mark clearly visible in the detail shown), but the raised surfaces were hand-polished.

Exposition Internationale des Arts Décoratifs Industriels et Modernes', after which it became known worldwide.

Vases

In the 1920s Lalique designed more than 200 vases, and a 150 bowls. They were intended more for decoration than for actual use. The vases were decorated in relief with realistic natural decoration; they include a mistletoe vase, a vase with grasshoppers perched on reeds (which was one of the earliest and most popular designs), vases with Bacchanalian dancing ladies, heavy vases in blueish opalescent glass with figures modelled in relief, a milky white vase with thistle decoration, a vase decorated in the Egyptian style with eucalyptus leaves, a vase with a frieze of mermaids in low relief, a vase with archers aiming at birds of prey, a vase with swimming fish, and one with stylized ferns. There were many patterns and the vases were executed in different kinds of glass. From a collector's point of view there is a considerable difference between a vase in coloured frosted glass, and the same model in brownish-blue opalescent glass. Some models were also done in coloured glass, either blue, amber, green or red, and black Lalique is the colour most prized by collectors today. The most important reference book for Lalique collectors is the 100-

page catalogue published by the firm in 1932. Over 1000 objects are illustrated here with their exact dimensions and model numbers. In addition the catalogue gives a good deal of information about the various colours in which models were available. As the catalogue is now itself a rare collector's item, collectors must satisfy themselves with photographic reprints, and even these seem to change hands at inflated prices.

Sculpture

Lalique had already made sculptures in miniature during his days as a jeweller. He decorated many of his jewels with finely sculpted figures in relief, either in ivory or in *Pâte de Verre*. He used the experience and stylistic asssurance gained during that time for the glass-sculptures designed by him during his Art Deco period. These sculptures were an important part of his glass production at that time. One of the most outstanding mass-produced figures of this period was his *'Suzanne au Bain'* (plate 116) - a naked female figure standing in a provocative pose against a background of finely modelled drapery. The style of this model was typical of the neo-classical taste of the 1920s. Another model in the vein was Model no. 835 *'Grand Nue'* and Model no. 837 *'Source de la Fontaine'*. This last is also a

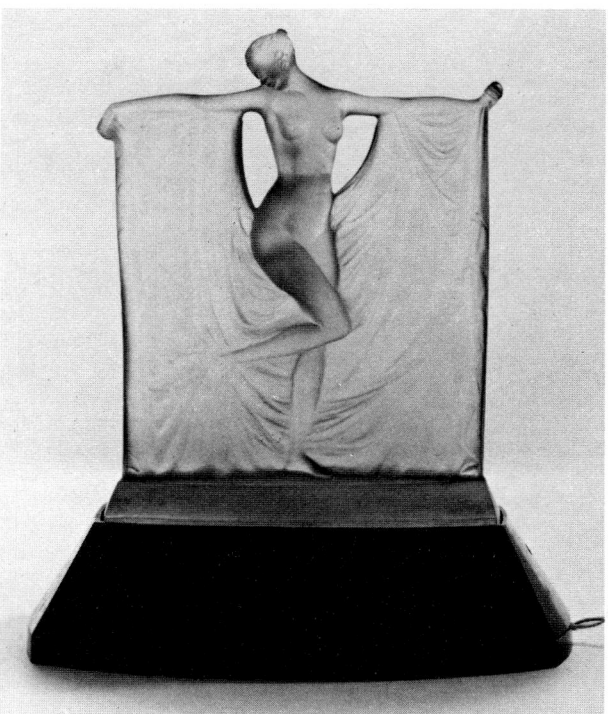

116 *'Suzanne au Bain'* by René Lalique. Opalescent glass figure illuminated from below by a light fitment concealed in a specially designed bronze mount, No. 833. Height 27.5 cm, *c.* 1920-34.

stylized figure, though more medieval than classical in style. As an optional extra it was possible to buy a special bronze base for most of the figures with a concealed light socket (also designed by Lalique) so that the figures could be lit from below. Lalique was particularly interested in the idea of 'light sculptures' and his most famous include *'L'Oiseau de Feu'* ('The Firebird') and two large fish sculptures.

Car Radiator Mascots

The car radiator mascots Lalique produced during the 1920s have a fascination all of their own. Plate 110 shows a group which includes some of his largest and most beautiful models. The figurehead with a stylized mane of wind-swept hair is a sort of 'Tutankhamun' of the motor-age. In English it was called 'Spirit of the Wind', which captures the intended mythological connotations. 'The Eagle's Head' mascot is more realistic in style (it is Model no. 1138 and known in French as *'Tête d'Aigle'*); it is incidentally said to have been presented by Adolf Hitler to some of his generals. The 'Large Dragonfly' mascot is a little

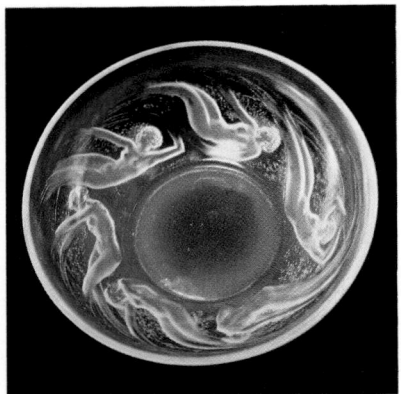

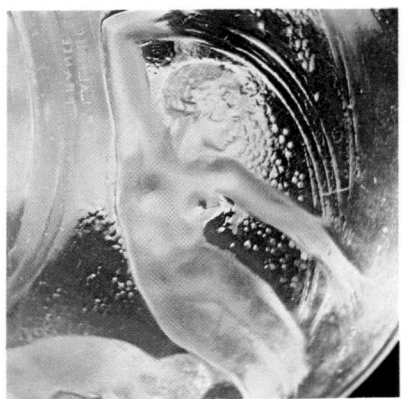

grotesque in style but very effective (this is Model no. 1145 *'Grande Libellule'*).

This concept of ornamental car-mascots was an exciting new idea, and *Studio* magazine devoted a whole article to these figures in 1931.

In 1925, Lalique was commissioned by the French car firm of Citroen to design a mascot for the new '5 *chevaux*'.

Appropriately Lalique designed one with five leaping horses. In the 1952 catalogue there are various illustrations of car mascots; there is the falcon's head, the ram's head, the small dragon-fly, the cockerel, and mustang, the peacock and the archer.

It has become fashionable to collect car-mascots and the prices for any in good condition - many of them have suffered slight damage and have been ground down at a later stage in order to try and hide imperfections - have been rising

sharply over the past few years. Apart from condition another important factor for the collector to consider is the colour of the glass of which they are made. The 'finish' of the clear models too makes a difference in value; the most sought-after finish is one where the glass has a pale amethyst tint.

Many of the mascots were intended to be lit from below, and some of them are found still mounted in their original radiator caps.

Glass Jewellery

Glass jewellery, particularly pendants with raised decoration became fashionalbe in the early 1920s. Lalique was one of the best known manufacturers of this style of jewellery, and another was the firm of Almaric Walter in Nancy which was known for its *pâte de verre* products. Most of the designs on these pendants refer back to the plant forms of the Art Nouveau

117 *'Ondines'* (Mermaids). Opalescent blue bowl decorated in relief with mermaids. Signed 'R. Lalique, France'. Diameter 27.5 cm, c. 1925.

118 Detail of 117.

119 *'Le Jour et la Nuit'* (Day and Night). Solid glass clock surround, decorated in deep relief, on bronze mount containing concealed light-fitment, No. 728. Signed in the glass 'R. Lalique'. Height 39 cm, c. 1920.

period. But there were also pieces with painted enamel decoration (see plate 126) like those of Marcel Goupy and Auguste Claude Heiligenstein.

Scent bottles

Stylishly designed scent bottles were a popular 1920s fashion accessory and can make a charming collection today. The various perfume manufacturers tried to outdo one another with the designs of their perfume bottles. To the Art Deco collector they represent an object very typical of its time, and are very much a part of the fashion-concious spirit of the age. There was already a well-established tradition for perfume containers. Baccarat, Saint Louis, and also Stourbridge in England were among the many firms who had already been involved for a long time in their manufacture. At the turn of the century Gallé had become interested in the making of perfume flasks but not as a commercial venture which would be of interest to perfume manu-facturers. The great breakthrough for artist-designed perfume bottles came with Lalique's commission from Coty. The first Lalique designs were executed by Legras before Lalique started producing them at his own factory in later years. Lalique executed a specific design for each specific perfume and they were as elaborate and

suggestive as the names of the perfumes themselves, names like *'Ambre Antique'*, *'Stys'*, *'Cyclamen'* or *'L'Effleurt'*. Lalique, apart from designing for Coty, worked for D'Orsay, Roger & Gallet, Arys, Riguad, Vigny and Worth. Plate 125 shows the perfume bottle designed for a Roger & Gallet perfume called *'Le Jade'*. (Perfume bottles like this one fetch high prices at auction, despite the fact that French perfume manufacturers must have produced around 25 to 30 million scent bottles of one kind or another. Note that it is important to make sure if you are a collector of scent bottles that you have the correct stopper intended for a particular bottle, as the stopper was an integral part of the design).

Lalique made stoppers of all kinds, some depicting female nudes, others with serpents' heads, buds, birds, insects or sometimes floral sprays that made the bottle look like a vase of flowers.

The bottles with elaborate stoppers are now the most expensive, as only a few have survived intact, obviously the stoppers, (particularly the delicately modelled ones) are usually far more vulnerable than the bottles themselves. Here too the 1932 Lalique catalogue is a useful reference book for collectors as it contains nearly 100 illustrations of scent bottles together with their descriptions.

120 Advertisement for Etling, from an art journal of the 1920s.

121 Advertisement for Sabino from an art journal of the 1920s.

122 Advertisement for Daum Nancy from an art journal of the 1920s.

Signatures and Marks

Almost every piece of Lalique is signed, with the exception of a few scent bottles specially designed for perfume manufacturers. There are both etched and impressed signatures. Usually the signature is 'R. Lalique' in bold capitals. If there is a number as well it refers not to a numbered edition but to the mould number. The R. is not present in signatures on pieces made after Lalique's death in 1945. Objects in current production bear the mark 'Lalique, France'.

Popular Art Deco

We have now dealt with the more sophisticated end of the market and Lalique's production ranging from car-mascots to rare vases, but there is also a lot of ordinary glass that is interesting. Much of the glass produced in vast quantities and never signed has many of the typical stylistic features of the period and is worth collecting. Such glass was made mainly in France or Bohemia, formed and an attractive feature of the 'Decorative Twenties'. Pieces such as those

123 The double-page illustration on the preceding pages shows Art Deco vases, decanters and perfume flasks, with stylized designs painted in coloured enamels. Signatures include Delvaux, H. Laroyer, France, Quenvit. Heights 8-30 cm.

which formed part of the collection of Martin Battersby (seen in plate 123) have 'great charm. This little group shows how a stylish collection of Art Deco glass need not depend on any of the big names. Wandering through the flea markets and junk shops picking out pieces for their distinctive shape or decoration can not only be great fun but rewarding - with the added attraction that no fortune is required to build up such a collection. A few suggestions might be helpful if one is looking for attractively designed mass-produced glass that is still considerably cheaper than Lalique. If you collect moulded glass look out for Sabino, Degues, Genet et Michon, Verlux, Etling or André Hunebelle. They all made what can be, and is often called, 'Lalique style' glass. Plates 120-122 are advertisements from contemporary magazines and show how glass firms laid emphasis in their publicity on the decorative qualities and latest styles of their wares; such glass was usually sold in department stores or boutiques. Apart from the frosted glass of the 1920s a quantity of coloured glass was manufactured; much of it was made in Bohemia but is unsigned and as yet unattributed. The French company Schneider was probably also responsible for the colourful range of glass known as 'Le Verre Français'. Verre Français glass is often not signed in full, but

124 A photograph from *Studio* Magazine, with decorative Art Deco glass.

has a distinguishing red, blue and white device worked into the glass. It is possible to build up a collection of these lesser known pieces quite cheaply. The colours predominantly used at the time were orange, mauve and yellow, and also a selection of bright mottled colours.

There were several other techniques in use at this time; one was deep-acid etching, and another a technique for producing a crackled effect. Crackled glass is sometimes referred to as 'ice-glass'. This 'crackled-ice' effect was achieved by dipping the molten glass in water at an early stage in the proceedings; this caused the substance to crack internally and left the appropriate effect on the finished piece. The 'crackled'

effect was used by Daum among others. When the desired cracking had taken place the glass was re-heated and worked into its final shape.

One of the styles peculiar to the period was that, already described, of glass blown into a wrought iron mount. On the whole these pieces were made by Daum and Majorelle who combined to manufacture such pieces. The glass used was usually coloured and blown into the mount in such a way that it seemed to bubble out past the restraining shapes of the rigid metal. Although vases of this kind can be a little uninteresting, it was a technique which was particularly effective

when used for making lampshades (see the example shown in plate 131).

In order to get a feeling for the period it helps to look at all aspects of decorative design during the 1920s and 1930s. Patterns for fashion textiles or colour schemes on carpets could equally well have been used on glass. The trained eye can pick out style whatever the

125 Lalique scent bottles. *From left to right*: *'Brule Parfum'*, and incense burner with moulded relief decoration of mermaids, *c.* 1925-30. *'Le Jade'*, green scent bottle designed for Roger & Gallet. Height 8 cm, *c.* 1927. 'Pan' perfume flask dating from 1932.

126 Costume jewelry in glass. *Left*: Two pendants in *pâte de verre* by Walter Nancy; *Centre*: bracelet (green) and pendant (with fish) by Lalique; *Right*: pendants with painted enamel designs by Goupy and Heiligenstein.

medium, and training is simply a matter of looking and learning. Money need not be the most important criterion for a collector. Two books which give an overall picture of the period can be strongly recommended. One is Paul Maenz's book *Art Deco Forms between the Wars* published by Du Mont in 1974 in Cologne, and the other Martin Battersby's *Decorative Twenties*, first published by Studio Vista in London in 1969. Battersby's book has become something of a classic and gives an excellent account of the period.

127 Cut-glass decanter with sun-burst motif, c. 1930.

128 Typical Art Deco scent bottles. Heights 8-15 cm.

Glass Lamps 1890-1930

Glass is the ideal material for decorative lighting. As the light shines through the various layers of cameo glass it vividly illuminates the flowers and landscapes in the design. The designs on the different layers of deep acid-etching stand out and come to life as light shines through them, and the larger the lamp, the more dramatic the effect. Crackled glass is also much enhanced by light shining through it.

Although *pâte de verre* lamps cannot give a particularly strong light they provide a warm, colourful glow. Leaded glass lamps in the style of Tiffany are transformed into illuminated paintings when lit: the principle is the same as in stained glass windows. The most spectacular leaded lamps of the period are by Tiffany himself. He was, incidentally, one of the first designers to experiment with the decorative possibilities of electric light. He worked with Thomas A. Eddison, the inventor of the light bulb, on a commission to decorate the interior of the Lyceum Theatre, and it was on this occasion that he carried out his first important experiments in decorative lighting. His later work, and that for which

he is best remembered today, seems a logical development of his earlier projects, for before manufacturing lamps, he spent many years designing massive stained glass pictures in the manner of stained glass windows. As Tiffany recalls in his memoirs, his lamps were just a convenient sideline in the beginning and the curved shades of the lamps were merely a variation on the flat surface of his pictures. His first catalogue of lamps appeared in 1898, and at this stage the lamps were comparatively simple; but they gradually became more elaborate with models like the magnificent Wisteria lamp or the jewel-like Dragonfly lamp. The designs were strong and assured, and the subject matter made these lamps very much a part of Art Nouveau.

Gallé Lamps

Gallé's first experiments using cameo glass for lighting were carried out before 1900 in Nancy. To him lighting, far from being a practical and functional concept, was atmospheric and full of symbolism. He saw it as a means of giving new expression to his art form. 'La

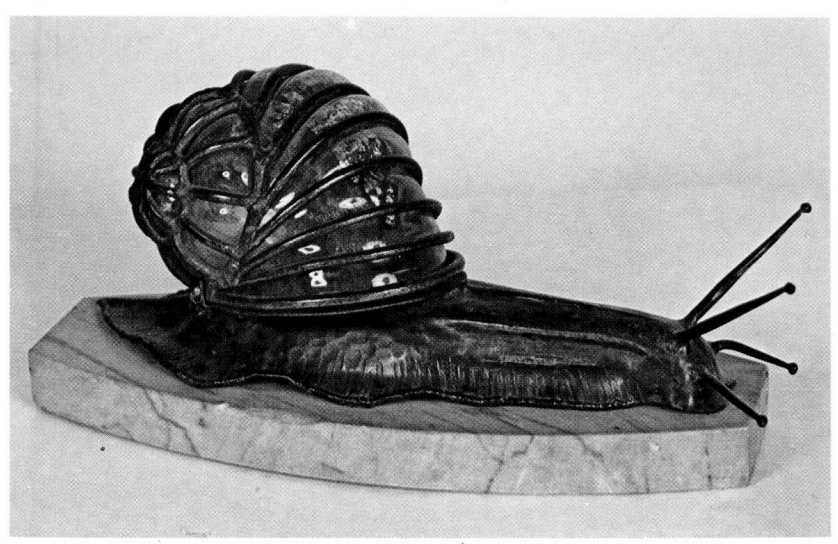

131 Table lamp
by Daum and
Marjorelle,
Nancy. The
base, in bronze
and wrought
iron is by
Marjorelle, and
the mottled
glass shade by
Daum,c.1900.

129 Tiffany
lamp with lotus-
blossom design.
Height 65.5 cm.

130 Lamp in the
form of a snail
by Chapelle
with glass by
Muller (Luné-
ville). The
coloured glass
was blown
through the
metal frame-
work, c.1900
work, c.1910

Vérité s'illuminera comme une lampe', he declared, 'The truth will shine like a light'. This was inscribed on one of his earliest lamps and was intended as a moral judgement on his view of the Dreyfus affair. The lamp was in the shape of a closed bud. It is typical Gallé's work and a fine example of his ambitions to combine language, sentiment and creative force.

The more ordinary Gallé cameo lamps were similar to the cameo vases. The base is simply an illuminated vase, and an inverted cameo bowl provides the shade, turning the whole into a conventional table lamp. The decoration is also similar to that of the vases; one sees the same colourful floral and landscape designs and the same decorative principles applied to lamps as to vases. The more valuable lamps have wheel-work on them, whereas the simpler models are just acid-etched. Like the vases, the simpler acid-etched models are referred to as '*Gallé industriel*'.

There are also, of course, cameo lamps which employ other techniques as well. Sometimes, for instance, the background is acid-etched while the detail is carved by hand. The lamps are signed in very much the same way as the vases. The most valuable of them are usually the ones with the most layers of glass and these have a vertical Gallé signature running from top to bottom; the more ordinary lamps, like the '*industriel*' vases, have a diagonal signature running from bottom to top.

Those lamps made after Gallé's death in 1904 are marked with a little acid-etched star before the signature. These are all commercial, and continued in production until 1931.

Gallé lamps have become a rarity, mainly because they are easily damaged and there is no way of restoring them if they are cracked in any way. The collector must make sure that base and shade were intended for one another. One often sees 'marriages' - lamps made up from a base and shade not originally intended for one another; these have very little value. Sometimes lamps appear on the market with cameo shades and wrought-iron bases, but these are highly suspect and often the wrought-iron part is merely a replacement for what was originally a cameo glass base. Wrought-iron bases with cameo shades, or cameo bases with fabric shades are almost always 'wrong'. There are however a few lamps designed by Daum and Majorelle (and even some by Gallé) where the base was originally intended to be wrought iron, but one should always by on guard and try to check the authenticity of such a piece by finding an illustration in a

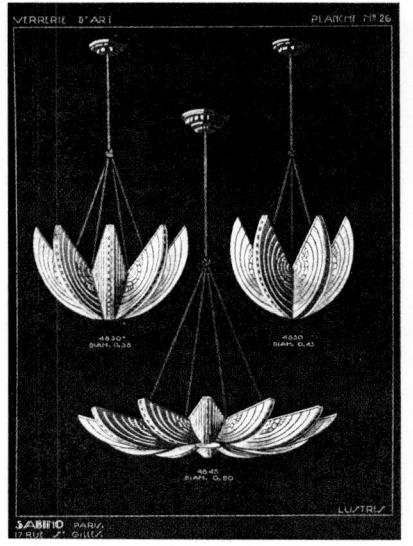

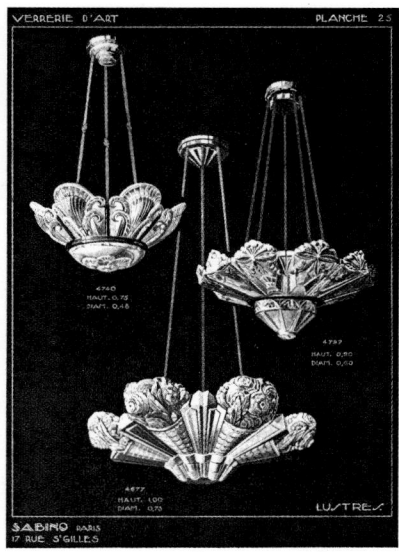

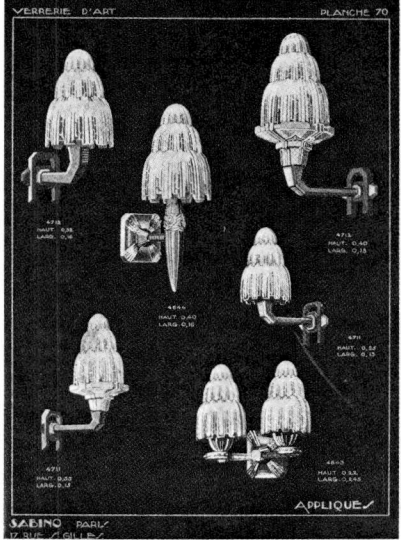

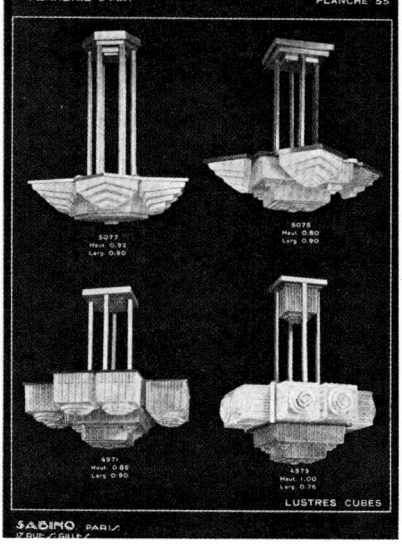

132 Photographs of frosted moulded-glass lampshades from the Sabino catalogue. This type of glass was particularly suited for lighting. It was used in wall-lights, ceiling fixtures and floor lamps by Lalique, Degues, Schneider, Muller, Etling and Sabino. The shades almost always have a moulded signature. Paris, c. 1925-30.

contemporary publication; for the chances are that it is merely an antique dealer's 'marriage of convenience'.

Reasonably priced lamps

With lamps as with vases, there is a considerable difference between the commercial product and the artist-designed piece, and this difference is reflected in current prices. Commercially produced lamps of the Art Nouveau and Art Deco periods can form an attractive collection. During the Art Nouveau period it was mainly Daum and Muller who manu-factured glass specifically for lighting, most of which was not cameo glass, but mottled coloured glass. This glass was built up in layers with metal oxide powder or coloured powdered glass inserted between each layer; when the glass was re-heated after the colour had been added, it took on the mottled effect, which makes for bright and

133 An 'industrial' Gallé Lamp, typical of those produced between 1900 and 1930. Height 48 cm.

134 Gallé lamp, polychrome cameo glass with carved flower decoration and foil inclusions. Height 50 cm, Nancy 1898.

135 *'Les Coprins'*, mushroom lamp by Emile Gallé, cameo glass ranging from two to five layers of glass, and foil inclusions, on a wrought iron base, Nancy 1904.

colourful glass lampshades.
This sort of glass was very popular for hanging lampshades and for small table lampshades. They were produced well into the 1930s and are usually found in combination with wrought-iron bases (in the case of table lamps) or wrought-iron frames (in the case of hanging lamps).

The French were responsible for most of the decorative light-fittings manufactured during the 1920s, and they completely ignored the German protestations about simplicity and functional design.

One can still find glass shades or glass lamps in good condition in

in plate 132 shows a page from an original Sabino sales catalogue with typical angular cubist shapes, stylized floral decoration, zig-zag designs, and the fountain motif. These lamps were usually made of milky, opaque glass mounted on chrome fittings. As a rule the makers name is impressed in the glass; this can hardly be called a 'signature', although dealers like to refer to the glass as 'signed'.

136 Lamps in carved cameo glass by Daum Frères, Nancy.

antique shops and antique markets today. There are plenty around by makers such as Degues, Sabino, Gonet et Michon, Schneider (otherwise known as *Verre Français)* and Muller Frères. The illustration

Information for the collector

Art and antique collecting have become very fashionable in the past few years. Collecting can become a fascinating pastime, the only draw-back being that the best things are fast disappearing from the market.

Until recently expert knowledge was confined to a small circle of connoisseurs, but with the recent craze for antiques there has been a wealth of research and Saturday browsers have become serious and informed collectors.

The situation nowadays is the reverse of what it was ten years ago. Today the collector is knowledgable about his subject, but finds it a struggle to build a collection. In years gone by finding things was easier, but it was far more difficult to identify and research them.

The basic qualities of glass

Gold and silver have a basic value, but this is not true of glass, which only has value as an art object or a household item.

Thus the most important considerations for the glass-collector are technical skill, style and an object's aesthetic appeal.

Date is important too. Also a piece of household glass, which in its time had no commercial value, can take on historical importance in retrospect.

Where value is concerned the main criteria are artistic, but condition is also of prime importance. Damaged glass seldom has any value. It is only in the very unusual or important examples of a particular sort of glass that a damaged piece will still be considered worthy of consideration. But as a general rule, any piece of glass that is either cracked, or damaged in any way, has hardly any value.

Maurice Marinot once appropriately remarked that the magic of glass lay in the cooling process, for that was when shapes and patterns established themselves. The collector will be mainly concerned with technical skill, innovation and artistic effects in which the unknown element of chance has had a part.

Glass itself never changes, it is the artist bringing his skills to bear on this most breakable of materials that lends each piece its own intrinsic charm.

Furniture can be restored from time to time, and it can even be modified, but glass manufacture is a once and forever process, which only endures until the glass finally shatters and breaks into pieces.

The rules of the art game

The antique trade has its own code of law. It is, of course, a case of 'some you win and some you lose'. One should always be conscious of trends and fashions in collecting, and check whether the objects you seek to buy or sell are on the way in or on the way out, because this can greatly effect the market.

It is the dealers with the largest stock who are in control, as they can either flood the market, or let things appear gradually, all of which has an effect on the price. Business depends on supply and demand within the trade, and the prices at auction give a good general idea of market trends.

Many thousands of pieces of glass go through the auction rooms in any one year; they are described in auction catalogues, and a study of these in combination with published price lists should leave one with a fair idea of the right price to pay to any given object. Even if a collector does not attend auctions, he may be sure that the value of any piece in his collection is being established every time a similar piece comes up for sale. One can tell from international auction price records whether a particular item is

going up or down in value, if a particular piece fetches £1000 at auction, a dealer will adjust his price accordingly. It is a strict rule of the art market that pieces must be exactly as they are described, because the catalogue description helps to set the price. And this is important when one considers that there are often large sums of money involved.

Museum collections are often a great help in identifying a piece, as are the special exhibitions that are frequently held in museums these days. Museums often choose a subject for an exhibition which they know to be popular on the art market, and conversely a museum exhibition can affect the price. When a similar piece is known to be in a museum collection, it helps the value of the object, as the trade is very conscious of what is or is not 'museum worthy'.

It is an established fact that the important centenary exhibition held in Darmstadt in 1977 caused a great revival of interest in German arts and crafts. Similarly the 1925 Exhibition held in Paris a few years ago renewed a taste for highly stylised Art Deco of the French sort, and the 1920s Berlin exhibition revived interest in the Bauhaus and functionalism.

When a piece is illustrated in a museum or exhibition catalogue, it somehow seems to legitimise it in the eyes of the collector.

Building up knowledge

It is most important that the collector should try to assimilate as much knowledge as possible. Much has been written on the subject of glass, and even if one only wants to purchase the occasional piece, it is well worth while acquiring some specialised knowledge. Specialist knowledge is essential for the buyer who is considering an expensive piece of Art Nouveau or Art Deco. It can be fascinating to find out about designers, decide whether one likes their style and whether they are important or not. It is also fascinating to investigate why and how an object was made in the first place, if it was exhibited and if so, whether it was considered rare and important at the time or just typical.

Specialised art books are a great help with the better objects, as the best pieces are usually described or illustrated, and comparison is therefore possible. It is advisable to be on the mailing list of a reputable book store dealing in art books so as to be able to keep up with the latest specialized publications.

Sometimes a piece in one's own collection is illustrated, which somehow seems to help justify the expense both of the object and the book in which it is illustrated! Some of the relevant publications are listed in the bibliography that follows and the section on how to build up a useful reference library. One cannot over-emphasise the importance of contemporary source material. Current publications are a great help, but it is a very good idea to browse in second-hand bookshops for books that might be relevant, and particularly for art journals of the period.

For dealer and collector alike it is important to try and keep in mind articles and illustrations from old periodicals. A photographic memory is invaluable when one is faced with a difficult decision about whether or not to buy, and is a short-cut to years of laborious researching. Thus looking through periodicals or art books can be good training for the eye, and one's subsequent knowledge serves one in good stead when it is a question of buying.

Art Glass as opposed to mass-produced glass

'Art Glass', as the name implies, is a cut above the ordinary. Prices for Art Glass are also proportionately higher.

The same degree of care is necessary in buying a piece of art glass as in buying a picture. Damage or restoration of any sort which might detract from the value of the piece, should be avoided if at all possible. If a piece of glass is not in any of the usual books, one should look for mentions of similar pieces; one might recall pieces by the same artist in museum collections. If not one can always browse through illustrations in contemporary art journals or auction catalogues in the hope of finding a parallel object. The artist's name alone does not determine the artistic value of a piece.

Both during the Art Nouveau and Art Deco periods it was customary for a piece of commercially produced glass to be artist-signed. 'Gallé Glass' however does not always mean glass that was hand-crafted by Gallé himself.

A parallel can be taken from the world of art-dealing. A painter decides to make a limited print edition based on one of his originals, say an edition of 300.

The original is by definition unique and priced accordingly - the parallel to this in the field of glass is the hand-wrought piece of art glass; this too can be called a *bona fide* 'original'. The limited editions can be compared to commercially produced models of glass which are more or less copies of an original. A signature on glass carries the same cachet as a signature on a painting. A signed piece is worth ten times more than an unsigned piece.

Commercial Art Nouveau and Art Deco glass often has instant appeal since it is both decorative and the finish is of good quality. By contrast, some of the more unusual hand-crafted originals might fail to impress at first sight and are something of an acquired taste.

Different kinds of glass and glassmaking techniques

A background knowledge of the different kinds of glass materials and the various techniques can save one from making mistakes. As the collector cannot just relegate a fake to his basement, as a museum might, a basic background knowledge is of vital importance to him if his collection is ambitious enough to include important pieces. It allows him to be objective in his judgement, so that he need not rely on the attributions of others or on the dealer's sales pitch. Even for the expert, attribution is often a matter of conjecture when it comes to glass.

The experienced collector does not need to look at signatures to determine the value of the more common kinds of art glass. When Art Nouveau first began to be collected, it was because it was attractive. In the early stages there were no reference books to help categorise objects. Perhaps this was what made collecting so pleasurable before so many reference books became available; indeed some of the most important collections were built up purely on instinctive judgement and based on a good eye and a feeling for the material.

What to collect

Collecting is a very personal matter, and each collection reflects the personality of its owner. A collection should not just grow, it should develop with each new acquisition along with the collector's expertise.

The last few years have proved that one can make a collection of almost anything, provided it is based on some idea that can be followed through. This is true of glass, where value certainly need not be the only criterion. One can for instance collect particular shapes; some collectors might stick to tall-necked vases others to long-stemmed wine glasses.

Twenty pieces are enough to give a collection its character. Once this has been established one can go on adding pieces. A good piece of advice to any glass collector is that rather than just collecting aimlessly, he should base his collection on a specific area.

Choosing a personal style

It is very rewarding for a collector to strike out in a new direction, rather than follow the main stream. As the scope is endless, it is advisable to specialise in some way however. Collecting is a matter of time combined with a little bit of luck.

The clever collector can group a series of chance finds into a collection with a basic shape. This is part of the joy of collecting, one begins by buying at random and later decides how the collection can proceed in a more definite direction.

There are all sorts of ideas for collecting: one can, for instance, collect car mascots, or miniature vases, or coloured liqueur glasses or glass jewellery, or glass lamps - there is no reason why a good collection of glass from this period has to be made up of Gallé, Tiffany or Lalique.

How objects change hands

Glass dealing has always been on an international level. The glass manufacturers produced their wares originally with the export trade in mind. Bohemian and Austrian glass was exported to America, England and France. Tiffany glass was exported from America to Europe, and one could buy Nancy glass in France, Germany or England. But what glass manufacturers once exported from their shores is now being re-imported by antique dealers. American dealers are looking for American glass in Europe, and European dealers for European glass in America. French glass is sent to Germany because it fetches better prices there.

Glass collectors soon realize that it is not always best to look for glass in the country of its origin. They will often find pieces in foreign countries (and even at lower prices). The best advice is to comb the world and never give up hope of achieving a 'coup'.

Signatures

Signature alone does not determine the value of an object, even though dealers would often have you believe that this is the case. Tiffany's signature was just a standard part of the manufacturing procedure and never done by his own hand. Even the most ordinary piece of commercially produced Gallé is signed, as a reminder that he himself had originally done a design for the model. But a signature is often just a trademark or something that was required by law if a piece was made for export. The best example of this is Loetz glass which was only signed if it was intended for export. Originally a signature was simply for identification purposes (although signatures have frequently been faked in recent years) - they are no indication of quality and certainly cannot be considered a price determining factor. It is overall quality, condition, workmanship, decoration and stylistic merit that

should all go towards evaluating a piece and an appropriate price.

Buying

The serious glass collector will become personally acquainted with leading auctioneers, art-dealers and experts. All these people will gladly give consideration to any serious enquiry. Buying at an auction is a public procedure and involves a certain element of showmanship. Sometimes auction houses are merely exchange markets with dealers and collectors auctioning their own merchandise to get the best price for it whilst at the same time buying more in order to replenish stock. Reserves can be placed on any item sold at auction; the mere fact that an item is up for sale is no guarantee that it will reach a satisfactory price. Glass collecting can be as much of a gamble as roulette.

Fakes, forgeries and imitations

The history of forgery is as old as the history of glass itself. Glass fakes are not as common as picture or furniture fakes, and this is due to the complexity both of the material itself, and of the techniques involved in working it. Glass can easily be ground, and a damaged vase be converted into a shallow bowl, or a damaged neck be ground smooth to leave a perfect sphere. The same goes for lamps. If the shade of a Gallé lamp gets damaged, the base can be converted into a saleable vase. One should always keep an eye open for possible conversions of this sort. There are apparently Japanese copies of Gallé vases which are difficult to distinguish from the originals. It is however difficult to believe this as the Gallé company's own attempts during the 1920s to maintain earlier high standards of cameo glass were not entirely successful. One also feels that such copies would hardly be a viable proposition economically because of the amount of work involved. It is more likely to find pieces that have been in some way 'improved'. For instance there are cases where a piece of French cameo glass by Muller or Daum has been 'transformed' into a piece by Gallé The expert will have no difficulty recognising such 'transformations'. It is not quite so obvious in the case of gold-lustre imitations of Tiffany. Some very successful gold lustre glass was made during the 1920s. But since then there have been alarmingly good Italian and American copies of Tiffany complete with signature and serial number. The inexperienced collector should be extremely careful to avoid pieces like this. Free-blown glasses by Koepping are often copied, as Koepping used a relatively simple technique. Koepping imitations appear fairly frequently on the market but are easy to pick out, although one needs to be fairly sure of what the originals looked like in case one mistakenly dismisses the original assuming it to be a fake. One should try and remember the exact shape and decoration of the originals and also the weight of the glass that was used to make them, and beware if one suspects minor variations that might have crept in during the copying process. Koepping is possibly the most forged of any glass designer.

Another frequent occurrence is fake signatures. This can produce strange hybrids such as when a piece of Loetz glass ends up with a Tiffany signature or a piece of Daum glass with a Gallé signature. On Sabino glass the signature is sometimes removed and replaced by a 'Lalique' signature. These signatures are only dangerous in the case of beginners or amateurs, for the professional will always think to check in the Lalique catalogue, if he suspects a piece of having a false signature.
So fake signatures are a worry only to the inexpert or one-time 'prestige' buyer, for whose benefit a large clear signature might have been prominently slapped on the side of a piece of glass. There are unfortunately a number of buyers who will be more easily impressed by a signature than by authenticity.

Price

Glass prices have become fairly
established, so that any known
piece of glass has more or less a
fixed market value. Prices for Art
Nouveau glass are no longer
speculative, since Art Nouveau has
become a safe investment. Art
Nouveau has in fact become rather
like the 'gilt edge' sector of the
stock market.
The price of glass is always
structured according to technical
skill. At one end of the market are
the unique artist-designed pieces,
that are real works of art, and were
expensive when they were made; at
the other extreme there is mass-
produced household glass which
was never intended to have any
artistic pretensions, but has since
become collected. There are many
categories of glass between the two
extremes. From a commercial point
of view the luxury end of industrial
glass production is the most
desirable, and fetches the highest
prices these days, commercially
produced pieces cannot be said to
have any historical importance, as
they are simply a part of a series.
What the manufacturer considered
good quality merchandise was
aimed at the upper middle classes
during the period of Art Nouveau;
today this constitutes good quality
merchandise for the antique dealer.
But even in this comparatively
stable market there can be
surprises.

The high price of industrial glass

The high quality and technical
finesse of turn-of-the-century art
glass makes it excellent merchandise
for the dealer today; this includes
glass from the Gallé factory in
Nancy, the better pieces of Daum,
pate de verre by Walter, and
standard pieces of Tiffany and
Loetz.
This kind of glass fetches high
prices, but there is no risk involved
in buying it if the quality is right.
The low risk element tends to
make the rise in price for such
glass gradual rather than sharp.
If one asks why this is so (and here
exceptions merely prove the rule)
then one stumbles upon one of the
most important rules of the trade.
Categorisation of quality dictates
stability of price, and where the
quality is predictable prices
resemble shares on the stock
exchange, the determining factor
being simply a description of the
quality.
The following criteria are important
for such categorization:
Provenance, shape, model, signature
and typical stylistic features.
These are the determing factors in
a commercial article.
A shortage of good merchandise on
the art market coupled with
increased demand, has been
responsible for the inflation of
prices over the last few years for

Glass shapes: Art Nouveau Wine glasses

Glass shapes: Table service

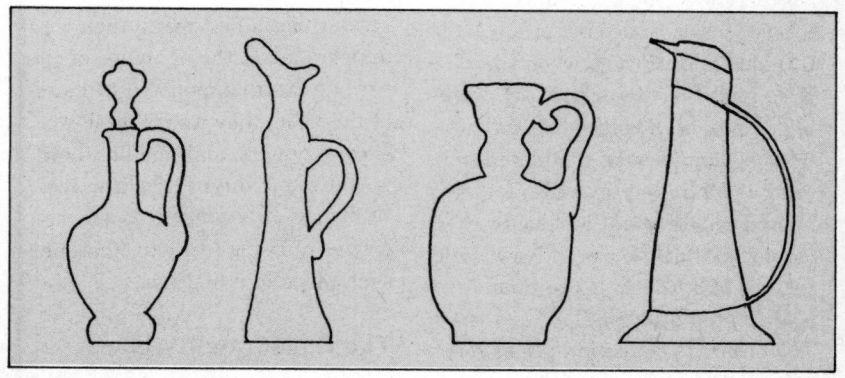

Glass shapes: Art Nouveau jugs

objects of this quality, but in no way does it reflect a re-appraisal of standards.

Average quality glass

Decent quality saleable merchandise. Minimum risk for buyer and seller. High initial cost with steady but not spectacular increase in value.

Important names in mass-produced glass

Standard Gallé, Standard Daum, *Pâte de verre* signed Walter, Standard Tiffany, Standard Loetz, commercially produced Lalique and Daum of the 1920s.

Unique pieces

The market for unique pieces, first experiments of important companies or major works by famous glass artists is quite different.

When a small Gallé marquetery vase (18cm in height) fetches £13,300 or a Daum vase £7,750, it is a reflection of artistic or technical merit. Even when they were made such 'works of art' were highly priced. For instance the famous Dennis vase completed in 1882 by John Northwood after many years of work, was sold through Tiffany & Co. in New York for $15,000, which at the time represented a fortune.

The original acquisition prices for Tiffany and Gallé are well known, thanks to contemporary records in museum files. Exceptional pieces of Tiffany cost several thousands of gold marks at the time. If pieces had manufacturing imperfections of any sort they were sold at reduced prices to museums and collectors. There is a close comparison in this respect with paintings and other works of art. The best glass was simply not found in every home during these periods; on the contrary these pieces were always highly priced to protect their exclusivity.

During the 1920s there was a similar situation, with Décorchemont and Marinot only selling their glass through the most exclusive interior designers in the world. The Gálle pieces illustrated in plate 71 show all the best features of turn-of-the-century art glass. To put together a similar group of vases these days would be a lengthy process and one can hardly imagine what it might involve in purely financial terms. When similar masterpieces first made their appearance at the openings of the various International World Fairs at the time, they were literally show-stoppers, and people would spend whole days discussing their brilliance. Nowadays it is a matter of being lucky to find one such piece in a lifetime.

The finest quality glass

Finest quality; works of art with only museum collections to compete against. Highest cost prices but also highest selling prices.

Famous examples

'Verrerie parlante' by Gallé, exceptional pieces by Tiffany, early pieces of *pâte de verre* by Décorchement, unique designs by Marinot, complicated flower goblets by Koepping and the more extraordinary pieces of glass by Daum Nancy.

Modestly priced glass

Modestly priced glass need not be unattractive. On the contrary there are many Art Nouveau and Art Deco pieces that are both pretty and decorative, and since these were mass-produced, they are affordable in present times. This sort of merchandise is still in plentiful supply, and can be purchased at reasonable prices in flea-markets, small antique shops and estate sales. The Paris flea-market is undoubtedly the best hunting-ground, and one also stands a good chance of finding things in the smaller shops in the provinces in France.

English prices are still the cheapest. There are a number of famous street-markets in London, and they are particularly good for finding the smaller type of 'antique'. In Belgium, Holland, Germany and Austria too flea-markets and antique shops have

opened up in many towns.

One should mention that most dealers are fairly well-informed about the merchandise they have in stock. Information is now readily available in the many excellent works of reference on the market and the antique dealer who does not known much about his stock today is rare.

As a result the small speculative dealer, running a small shop or stall in the flea market, will often over price rather than under price his goods. The wise buyer will therefore know and keep abreast of current going prices. Nonetheless while the smaller dealer may be less indiscriminate than he once was, bargains and good buys can still be found in such places.

Modest quality glass

Simple glass can be very decorative, but beware of over-pricing. Put together with taste, simple pieces can make an impressive collection.

Selected examples

Moulded Sabino, Etling & Degues, Art Deco glass with enamel painted decoration, Bohemian coloured faceted glass, W.M.F. glass, iridescent glass by Pallme-König and other Bohemian glassworks during the Art Deco period, long-stemmed Art Nouveau wine glasses, 1920s cocktail glasses.

Cameo glass with cut decoration

Description

Made up from several layers of coloured glass which are then carved in relief either with special tools or by wheel-cutting. A highly skilled and time-consuming technique.

Recognisable characteristics

Recognisable by its subtly modelled surface, and its fine colour shading produced by varied depths of cutting through the different coloured layers.

Special features

This technique is often used in conjunction with others such as etching, enamel-painting, gilding and iridescent effects.

Firms and artists

Léveillé, Legras, Loetz, Muller Frères, Gallé, Daum, Val St. Lambert, Vallerysthal, Burgen-Schverer & Co.

Examples

4/5/6/14/48/52/76/77/78/83/97/99/100/134

Cameo glass with etched decoration

Description

A process whereby hydrochloric acid is used to erode parts of the surface to the required depths and shapes in order to provide decoration. The areas where decoration is not intended are coated with an acid-resistant lacquer.

Firms and artists

Léveillé, Legras, Goldberg, Loetz, Muller Frères, Val St. Lambert, Vallerysthal, Burgen, Schverer & Co., Moser Karlsbad.

Examples

49/70/79/80/81/84/85/86/87/91/92/93/94/95/96/133

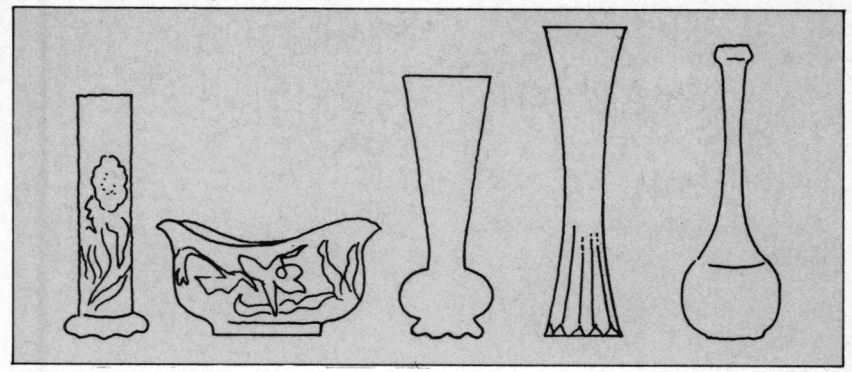

Glass shapes: Gallé vases

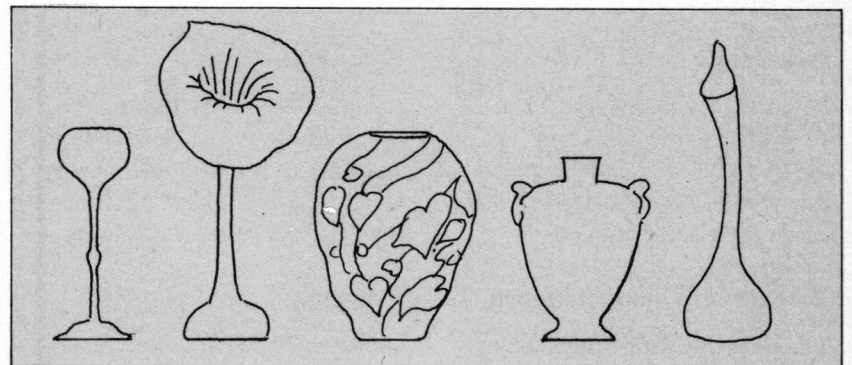

Glass shapes: Tiffany vases

Glass shapes: Loetz vases

Recognisable characteristics

Surface decoration; softly carved lines and slightly porous looking body.

Special features

Can be combined with some hand-cut and enamel decoration.

Enamel Painting

Description

Enamel colours cold-painted onto the surface of the glass and then fired on at medium temperatures. One should differentiate between transparent and opaque paint.

Recognisable characteristics

The layer of colour is normally applied in such a way as to provide lightly raised decoration.

Special features

Signatures are often also enamel-painted.

Firms and artists

Daum, Gallé, Muller Frères, Legras, Vallerysthal, Heckert, Haida and Steineschonau Trade schools, Lalique, Marinot, Heiligenstein, Goupy, *Verre Français*, Delvaux

Examples

16/40/41/70/88/101/126

Iridescent and lustre glass

Description

By either throwing metal salts over the hot surface of a piece of glass or passing the glass through

Firms and artists

Duc de Caranza, Schmoll von Eisenwerth, Poschinger, Schneckendorf, Pantin, Stumpf, metallic steam, shimmering surface films can be deposited to give metallic lustres ranging from red, green, blue or yellow to silver or gold on the surface of a glass.

Recognisable characteristics

A thin metallic film on the surface of the glass.

Special features

Iridescence can also be applied to transparent glass, when this takes on a rainbow like sheen.

Touvier, Violett & Co., Loetz, Pallme-König, Tiffany, Quezal, Steuben, W.M.F.

Examples

12/13/18/20/21/22/23/25/29
30/31/32/33/34/35/36/44/56
59/60/61/63/64/65/67/68/69

Moulded glass

Description

Made by pressing a precisely measured amount of glass into a metal mould under pressure. The mould is in several pieces to enable the glass to be removed.

Recognisable characteristics

Moulded glass is always recognisable by the seams left on the glass by the joins in the mould. Signatures are usually a part of the mould.

Special features

Made in all colours and frequently given a matt acid or sand-blasted surface finish.

Firms and artists

Lalique, Sabino, Hunebelle, Degues, Daum.

Examples

1/2/110/111/114/115/116/117/
118/119/120/121/122/125/127/
128/132

Pâte-de-verre

Description

Made by incorporating ground glass in a paste into which coloured powder is mixed; this is then shaped and fired at high temperatures. The annealing (cooling) process has to be carefully controlled to prevent surface cracking.

Recognisable characteristics

A solid, deeply coloured material with a rather porous looking surface.

Special features

The techniques of *'pâte d'émail'* and *'pâte de cristal'* are similar to *pâte-de-verre*, all of them closely related to ceramic techniques.

Firms and artists

Daum, Cros, Walter, Argy-Rousseau, Dammouse, Décorchement, Despret.

Examples

70/71/102/103/104/105/106/107/108/109/126

Metal-foil inclusions

Description

Art Nouveau glass makers used foil inclusions in the same way as the Venetians had done. The thinnest gold-leaf was inserted into the glass during the process of manufacture.

Recognisable characteristics

Fine pieces of metal foil visible beneath the glass surface.

Firms and artists

Gallé, Rousseau, Léveillé, Daum, Tiffany.

Examples

76/130/134/135

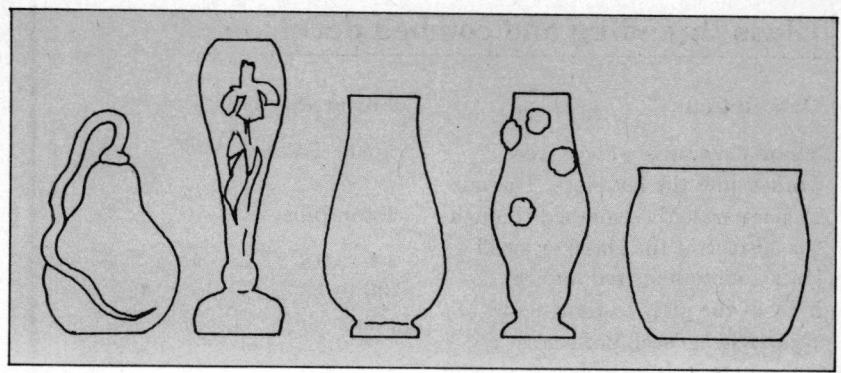

Glass shapes: Daum vases

Glass shapes: Bohemian Art Nouveau glass

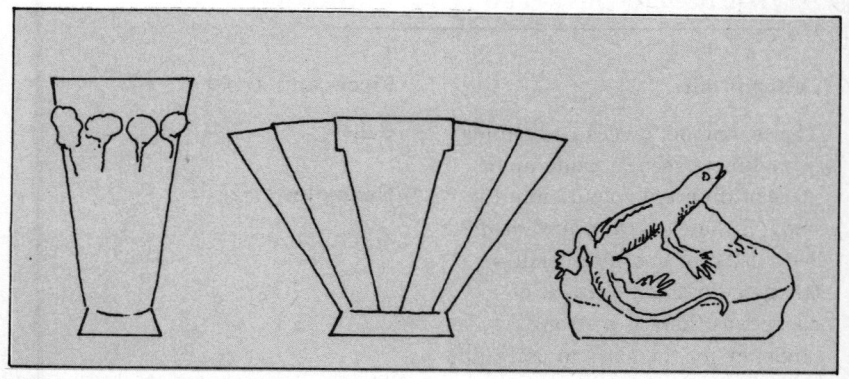

Glass shapes: *Pâte de Verre* objects

Glass threading and combed decoration

Description

These decorative effects were worked into the hot glass. Threads of glass are either combed through the surface of the glass, or small glass splinters melted into the body of the glass to form a sort of *'pointilliste'* overall pattern; or a web of glass-threading is spun onto the surface which does not melt into it, but cools before the body of the glass itself and stands out in relief.

Recognisable characteristics

Overall silvery spots fused into the surface of the glass, colourful internal feathering, or applied thread decorations.

Firms and artists

Loetz, Pallme-König, Tiffany

Examples

12/13/18/27/28/29/30/31/32/ 33/36/53/54/55/56/59/60

Marqueterie-de-verre (Glass marquetry)

Description

The technique involes embedding or melting a section made up of glass of different colours into the body of the glass. *Marqueterie-de-verre* calls for enormous skill combined with an element of chance, as there is a strong tendency for the glass to crack due to tensions built up during the cooling process.

Firms and artist

Gallé

Examples

4/5/70/76/82/89

Recognisable characteristics

Resembles wood marquetry work but can easily be confused with ordinary carved cameo glass when there is carving over and above the marquetry.

Special features

A large number of Gallé's unfinished pieces (i.e. ones that cracked whilst cooling) of *marqueterie-de-verre* were marked *'Etude'*. Because these pieces were left unfinished they offer a fascinating insight into the glass maker's art.

Millefiori glass

Description

Decoration is made by fusing different coloured glass rods. The rods are in bundles which are then melted into the body of the glass to make colourful patterns.

Recognisable characteristics

Multi-coloured dots or stripes underneath the surface of the glass. The patterns are usually floral.

Special features

Millefiori decoration was sometimes used in vases, in much the same way as in paperweights.

Firms and artists

Tiffany, Baccarat, *'Verre Français'* (red, white and blue millefiori threads in place of a signature).

Example

66

Lamp blown glass

Description

Figurines and decorative vases shaped over a burner flame from coloured glass rods. This technique is a simple home-craft.

Recognisable characteristics

Delicately wrought pieces in a wide range of colours.

Special features

The simplicity of this technique has led to a number of forgeries.

Firms and artists

Karl Koepping, Friedrich Zitzmann

Example

42

Powdered glass inclusions

Description

The roughly shaped glass is rolled in particles of metal oxide or a powder made of coloured ground glass and then re-fired so that the powder becomes incorporated.

Recognisable characteristics

Clouded colour effects either on or underneath the surface.

Special features

This technique was also used in conjunction with cameo glass, etching and enamel painting. It was particularly popular for the manufacture of lamps.

Firms and artists

Daum, Décorchemont, Walter, Despret, Argy-Rousseau

Examples

70/93/94/97/131

149

Glass Shapes: Moulded glass of the 1920s

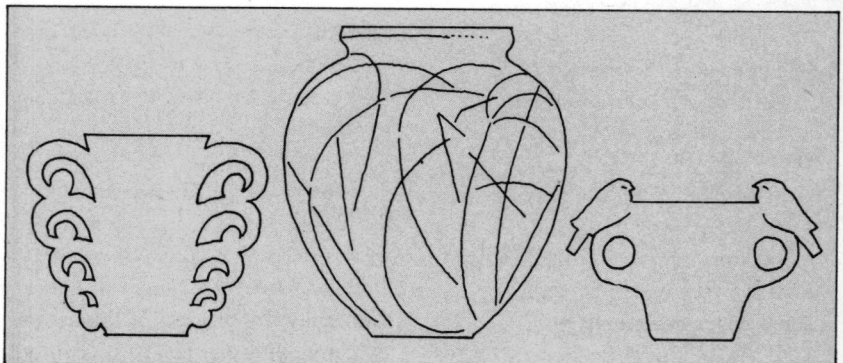

Glass shapes: Lalique glass

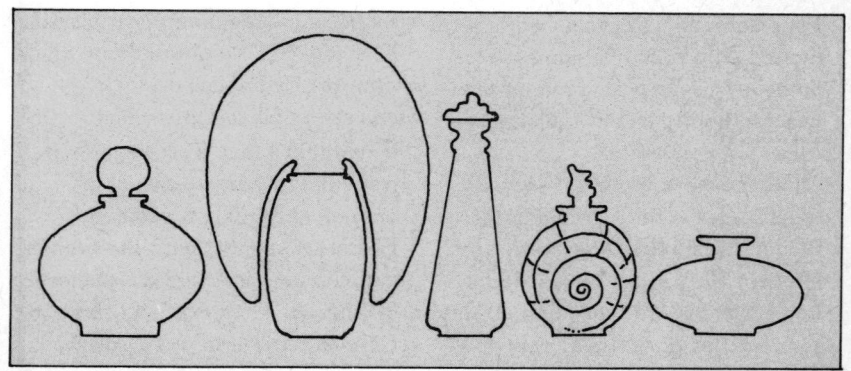

Glass shapes: Scent bottles

Building up a reference library

Documentary evidence is of the greatest importance for the glass collector and he will therefore do what he can to build up a handy reference library as this can be of great help when making reliable attributions. All this is a significant part of collecting and is of particular use in helping with any . difficult decision as to whether or not to buy a particular piece.

It has come to be almost as difficult to find the reference material as to find the glass itself. One often has to be satisfied with photocopies, generally readily available at most libraries. Collectors reference books have become very expensive and in some cases extremely rare.

The most important work on Gallé was written in 1903 by Louis de Fourcaud and was published in a limited edition of 300 copies. This is the only source for some of the hitherto undiscovered Gallé pieces.

Another rare book that is much sought after is the German author Gustav Pazaurek's *Moderne Glaser* (*Modern Glassware*) published in Leipzig in 1901. It goes into all the complexities of contemporary glass production in great detail, giving not only extensive descriptions of

current techniques but also the history of all the important glass manufacturers. It has numerous illustrations and is considered one of the most important research documents. The later, 1925, edition of *Moderne Glaser* is just as hard to find and casts a more critical eye on the Art Nouveau period, also giving an account of art glass production of the 1920s. Such full and detailed description is not available elsewhere, particularly with regard to Bohemian glass manufacturers. Anybody interested in Bohemian glass of the period will have to rely almost exclusively on Pazaurek.

For the collector of Lalique the 1932 Lalique catalogue is of major importance as it contains descriptions of over 1500 pieces of glass. Generally the original of this is not available and one has to be content with a photocopy. Other important documentary evidence is to be found in contemporary art journals. The collector should find out which libraries have these on their shelves as no serious collector can do without them. The art journals were all fairly international in outlook and it is advisable to become aquainted with the French and German ones as well as those in English. The most important German periodical was *Deutsche Kunst und Dekoration*. Published in Darmstadt, it had a lot to say

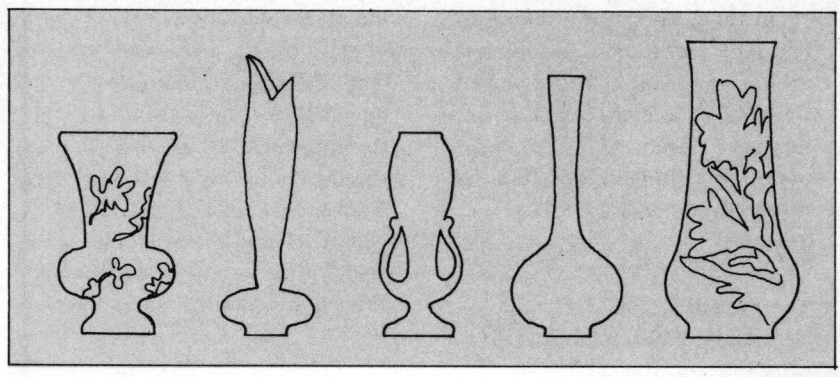

Glass shapes: Gallé vases

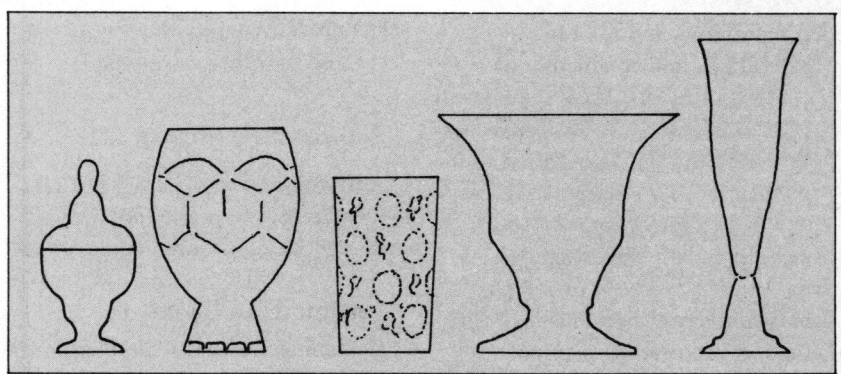

Glass shapes: Bohemian Art Nouveau glass

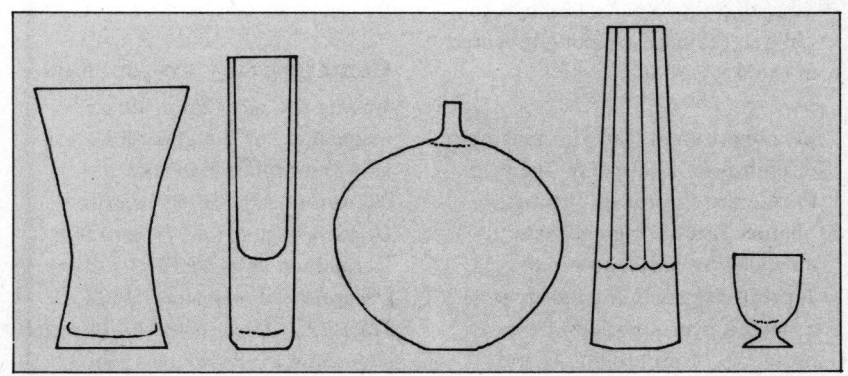

Glass shapes: Some 'new functionalist' forms

about the avant-garde exhibitions that took place there, including the exhibitions of interior design. When Gallé died the magazine did an extensive resume of his life and work and continued reporting the latest developments in glass design.

The French journal *Art et Décoration* is also important. It mentioned all the leading Art Nouveau and Art Deco artists, published the results of design competitions and did reviews of exhibitions and commentaries on contemporary art. It contains much of relevance for the glass collector as during the ten year period of its publication, a good part of it was devoted to the decorative arts including glass. The English publication *Studio* is one of the most important periodicals of the time. It reported fully (if not regularly) on all the developments in glass design. It was in this magazine that the first article on Lalique radiator mascots appeared in the early 1930s.

In trying to make attributions one often has no alternative but to go to reference libraries and take photocopies of original texts. It may also be useful to get the appropriate auction catalogues. If collected over a period of time these can often provide useful information, as they describe and illustrate many thousands of pieces of glass over a period of a year. The catalogues of the major auction houses can be strongly recommended as can their catalogues for specialist Art Nouveau and Art Deco sales in New York and Monaco. The same goes for the catalogues of the big French and German auctioneers.

The collector should order museum and exhibition catalogues in good time because bitter experience has proved how quickly these sell out and become unavailable.

A reference library

A useful reference library should include contemporary publications as well as modern reference books.

Antiquarian books

Contemporary books like Pazaurek's *Moderne Glaser* Leipzig 1901 are of enormous help. If unobtainable, photocopies can be recommended.

Contemporary art journals

Among the most important magazines for the glass collector are: *The Studio Yearbook of Decorative Art*, 1906 onwards, *Deutsche Kunst und Dekoration*, Darmstadt 1897-1934, *Art et Décoration*, Paris 1897-1938, *Mobilier et Décoration*. All of which should be available at a good reference library.

Catalogues

A number of larger firms published catalogues. The Lalique catalogue is essential, and the Daum Nancy, Tiffany, Sabino and Val St. Lambert catalogues can also come in useful.

Auction catalogues

For a number of years now many of the important European auction houses (Christie's King Street, London; Christie's Park Avenue, New York; Sotheby's Belgravia, London; Sotheby's Park Bernet, New York; Wolfgang Ketterer, Munich; Maître Black, Adert, Picard, Trajan, Paris) have held specialist sales of Art Nouveau and Art Deco glass and other objects, always accompanied by an extensively illustrated catalgoue. These are worth collecting as they may well contain valuable documentary information.

Exhibition and commemorative catalogues

Again a useful source of well-researched information. A particularly good example is Erika Billeter's catalogue of the glass collection at the Bellerive Museum in Zurich.

Bibliography

Specialist monographs and general books on the period in English.

Victor Arwas, Glass - Art Nouveau to Art Deco, Academy Editions, London 1971

A comprehensive, well-illustrated book with alphabetically arranged entries on all the glass artists and glasshouses of the period (has a useful bibliography).

Martin Battersby, The Decorative Twenties, Studio Vista, London 1969

One of the first and most perceptively written books on the period, that catches the spirit of the age.

Martin Battersby, The Decorative Thirties, Studio Vista, London 1971

One of the few books on the decorative arts of this period.

Philippe Garner, Emile Gallé, Academy Editions, London 1976

An especially informative monograph on the most famous French Art Nouveau glass designer. It portrays him as an artist of considerable talent, an entrepreneur, both bourgeois and eclectic. It is particularly recommended for its documentary illustrations and its choice of the very best Gallé pieces.

Ray and Lee Grover, Carved and Decorated European Art Glass, Tuttle, Rutland (Vermont) 1970.

A highly recommended, well-illustrated and concisely written book on the state of European carved glass at the turn of the century. The authors are collectors themselves and their commentary is therefore always interesting. The illustrations are well chosen to show all the most important pieces in European museums and private collections.

Robert Koch, Louis C. Tiffany, Rebel in Glass, Crown, New York 1964

Basic book on Tiffany and his art with many illustrations and an informative text.

Alain Lesieutre, The Spirit and Splendour of Art Deco, Two Continents, New York/ Paddington Press, London, 1975

A book on the more luxurious aspects of Art Deco.

Katherine Morrison McClinton, Lalique for Collectors, Scribner's, New York/ Lutterworth Press, Guildford, 1975

One of the first books to make a comprehensive survey of Lalique's jewellery as well as his other glass. Strongly recommended to collectors for its all-round grasp of the subject. The objects are arranged according to category.

Keith Middlemas, Continental Coloured Glass, Barrie & Jenkins, London, 1971

A richly illustrated book of the history of coloured glass from Venetian to Art Nouveau.

Albert Christian Revi, Nineteenth-Century Glass, Nelson, New York, 1959

A manual on glass production and techniques completely written and full of reliable information on this very important aspect of glass.

In French

Janine Bloch-Dermant, L'Art du Verre en France 1860-1914, Edita, Lausanne, 1974

A well-illustrated, detailed book with comprehensive stylistic and technical descriptions of the major glasshouses.

Yvonne Brunhammer, Le Style '25, Baschet, Paris 1976.

An illustrated survey of the best of Art Deco in European collections.

Laurence Buffet-Challié, Le Modern Style, Baschet, Paris 1976

An illustrated survey of the best of Art Nouveau in European collections.

Maurice Rheims, L'Art 1900 - ou Le Style Jules Verne, Arts et Métiers Graphiques, Paris 1965

An important, comprehensive and well-written book on decorative arts at the turn of the century.

In German

Albrecht Bangert, Lampen 1890-1930, Heyne, Munich 1978

A comprehensive survey of artistic lighting. A profusely illustrated pocket-book.

Helga Hilschenz, Das Glas des Jugendstil, Prestel Verlag, Munich 1973

A well-illustrated catalogue of the Hentrich Collection in Dusseldorf. The text contains many detailed descriptions and explanations of terms. It is an important reference work with particularly useful illustrations.

Paul Maenz, Art Deco 1920-1940, Du Mont Schauberg, Cologne 1974

A brilliantly written book on life styles between the two World Wars.

Waltraud Neuwirth, Das Glas des Jugendstils, Prestel Verlag, Munich 1973

A catalogue based on the glass collection in the Museum fur Kunst und Gewerbe, Vienna, and compiled with typical German thoroughness.

Wolf Uecker, Lampen und Leuchter - art nouveau art deco, Herrsching 1978

Typical light fixtures by important artists and glass companies. Illustrated in colour.

Museums and Collections

AMERICA
Corning (N.Y.)
The Corning Museum of Glass
Corning Glass Center
Catalogue: *Glass from the Corning
Museum of Glass. A guide to the
Collections.*
New York:
The Metropolitan Museum of Art,
Fifth Avenue / 82nd Street. N.Y.

AUSTRIA
Vienna
Osterreichisches Museum fur
angewandte Kunst, Stubenring 5.
Vienna.
Catalogue: Waltraud Neuwirth,
*Sammlung des Osterreichischen
Museums.*

BELGIUM
Liège
Musée du Verre,
13 quai de Maastricht

FRANCE
Paris
Musée des Arts Décoratifs,
107-109, rue de Rivoli

Nancy
Musée de l'Ecole de Nancy,
36-38, rue du Sergent Blandan.

GREAT BRITAIN
London
The Victoria and Albert Museum,
Cromwell Road, SW7.
The Bethnal Green Museum,
Cambridge Heath Road, E2.
The Victoria and Albert Museum
holds the museum's collection of
historical glass and the Bethnal
Green Museum exhibits the
museum's collection of Art Nouveau
glass. Both closed on Fridays.

GERMANY

Darmstadt
Hessisches Landesmuseum,
Friedenplatz 1.
Catalogue: *Kunsthandwerk um
1900, Jugendstil, Art Nouveau,
Modern Style.*
Catalogue: *Glas Kunst*, No. 1.,
edited by Gerhard Bott.
Düsseldorf
Kunstmuseum Düsseldorf,
Ehrenhof 5.
Catalogue: Helga Hilschenz, *Das
Glas des Jugendstils*, Munich, 1973.
Frankfurt
Museum fur Kunsthandwerk,
Schaumainkel 15.
Hamburg
Museum fur Kunst und Gewerbe,
Holstenwall 24.
Hanover
Kästner Museum,
Tranplatz 3.
Catalogue: *Glassamlung -
Bildkatalog 11,* edited by Christa
Mosel.
Munich
Museum Stuck-Villa,
8 Munich 80,
Prinz-Regentenstrasse 60.

SWITZERLAND

Zurich
Museum Bellerive - Sammlung des
Kunstgewerbe Museums,
Hoschgasse 3.
Catalogue: Erika Billeter, *Glas aus
der Sammlung des Kunstgewerbe
Museums in Zurich*, 1969.

Auction houses which hold sales of Art Nouveau and Art Deco glass

Christie's, 8 King Street, St. James's, London SW1.
Christie's hold between three and
four annual sales of Art Nouveau,
Art Deco and Studio Pottery,
which includes fine pieces of art
glass predominately by Gallé and
Lalique. Christies also hold regular
sales in Monaco and New York,
where Tiffany glass predominates.

Sotheby's Belgravia, 19, Motcomb St., London SW1.
This branch of Sotheby's chiefly
holds sales of Victorian and
twentieth-century applied arts with
regular sales of Art Nouveau and
Art Deco art glass.

Sotheby Parke Bernet, 980, Madison Avenue, New York 10021.
The American branch of Sotheby's
holds prestigious sales of Art

Nouveau and Art Deco glass,
especially by Tiffany. Each of
these auction houses publishes
comprehensive catalogues of their
sale of glass which can be had on
subscription.

Gallerie W. Ketterer, Prinzregentenstrasse 60. 8000 Munich 80.

Ketterer's hold two annual auction
sales of Art Nouveau and Art
Deco, the high point of which are
the pieces of glass. A well-
illustrated catalogue is issued for
each sale and can be had on
subscription.

Hôtel Drouot, Quai d'Orsay, Paris.
A large number of auction sales
take place here, but, unlike
Christie's or Sotheby's, Hôtel
Drouot hold few specialized sales.
Information about sales held here
can be obtained from the *Gazette
de l'Hôtel Drouot*, Redaction 37,
rue la Fayette, 75009 Paris.

Index

Page numbers in italics
refer to illustrations

Index

160

Acknowledgements:

Paris:
Mr and Mrs Walker, Paris
41/71/76-78/82/83/112/135
Jean François Manières, Paris 134
Jean-François Parry, Paris
80/81/101/131/133
Christian Sapet, Paris 130

London:
Christie's, King Street, London 55
Sotheby's Belgravia, London
14/58/59/60/66/68/69/102/109/
111/116/119/123/127/128
M. Pruskin, London 16/125/126
Collection Jack Pacifico, London 53
Bob Lawrence, London 110/126
John Jesse, London 51
Mikael Hallström, London 1/110/126
Dan Klein Ltd 54

Munich:
Auktionshaus Ketterer, Munich
12/13/18/20/22/23/33-36/49/53/
54/55/56/61-65/67/74/79/84-92/94
96/99/100/103-108/114/115/117/118
Museum Stuck-Villa, Munich
70/97/129
S. von Spaeth, Munich
40/43/45/46/47/50

Nancy:
Musée de l'Ecole de Nancy 72

Wurtzburg:
Kunsthandel Jana 39

Publications:
Pazaurek, *Moderne Glaser*,
Leipzig 1901
*Art et Décoration, Deutsche Kunst
und Dekoration* and others:
3/4/5/6/7/8/9/10/11/17/19/37/38/
42/48/75/98/113/120/121/122/
124/132/136